Project Management Institute

REQUIREMENTS MANAGEMENT:
A PRACTICE GUIDE

Library of Congress Cataloging-in-Publication Data

Names: Project Management Institute, issuing body.
Title: Requirements management : a practice guide.
Other titles: Requirements management (Project Management Institute)
Description: Newtown Square, Pennsylvania : Project Management Institute,
   Inc., [2016] | Includes bibliographical references.
Identifiers: LCCN 2015040239| ISBN 9781628250893 (pbk. : alk. paper) | ISBN
   1628250895 (pbk. : alk. paper)
Subjects: LCSH: Project management.
Classification: LCC HD69.P75 R465 2016 | DDC 658.4/04--dc23 LC record available at http://lccn.loc.
gov/2015040239

Published by: Project Management Institute, Inc.
                 14 Campus Boulevard
                 Newtown Square, Pennsylvania 19073-3299 USA
                 Phone: +610-356-4600
                 Fax: +610-356-4647
                 Email: customercare@pmi.org
                 Internet: www.PMI.org

TABLE OF CONTENTS

PREFACE

Requirements Management: A Practice Guide is a complementary document to the Project Management Institute's (PMI's) foundational standards. This practice guide provides guidance for project and program managers who are looking to further understand the components and importance of requirements management.

Industry has generally accepted that a requirements process will encompass the tasks associated with requirements development and requirements management. To establish a consistent understanding of the terms, each is defined. Requirements development encompasses the tasks of: eliciting and identifying requirements, planning, analysis, documenting or specifying requirements, and validating and verifying requirements.

Requirements management entails managing requirements of the project's products and product components and ensuring alignment between those requirements and the project's plans and work products. Requirements management therefore encompasses the tasks of: establishing a requirements baseline, and maintaining traceability, change control, and configuration management.

Business analysis includes two additional components to requirements development and requirements management. Those components include needs assessment, which begins pre-project/program, and solution evaluation, which occurs before and after solution implementation.

Historically, PMI included the tasks of requirements development and requirements management within requirements management, but with the 2014 introduction of *Business Analysis for Practitioners: A Practice Guide* and the PMI Professional in Business Analysis (PMI-PBA)® certification, PMI is standardizing on the term and definition of "business analysis" as a critical competence for project, program, and portfolio management, and will use the term "requirements management" as a component of business analysis.

For this reason and our stakeholders' requirement for a stand-alone document, readers of this guide who are familiar with *Business Analysis for Practitioners: A Practice Guide* will recognize and appreciate the consistencies between the two practice guides, especially in the sections addressing Needs Assessment, Planning, Elicitation, Analysis, and Solution Evaluation.

Practice guides are intended to encourage discussion related to areas of practice where there may not yet be consensus. Requirements development and requirements management practices have been performed for a long time, yet these practices continue to evolve and grow as indicated in the 2014 PMI *Pulse of the Profession*® *In-Depth Report* titled *Requirements Management: A Core Competency for Project and Program Success*. The report states that 52% of organizations expect an increase in the integration of requirements management and business analysis with project management over the next 3 to 5 years and that 58% of organizations are focusing on more defined practices and processes.

PMI is introducing this practice guide to act as the bridge between project management as specified in *A Guide to the Project Management Body of Knowledge (PMBOK*® *Guide) –* Fifth Edition and business analysis as specified in *Business Analysis for Practitioners: A Practice Guide.* PMI research indicates that 67% of high-performing organizations value the collaboration between project managers and business analysts or whatever role is responsible for requirements-related activities. This guide is intended to endorse and support increased collaboration and understanding as a means toward attaining increases in project and program success.

As such, the primary audience for this guide is project and program managers who are more familiar with PMI's historical position on requirements management and less aware of business analysis and PMI's *Business Analysis for Practitioners: A Practice Guide.* The intended audience for *Business Analysis for Practitioners: A Practice Guide* is anyone who is responsible for performing business analysis work regardless of his or her title.

Practice guides are developed by leading experts in the field using a process that provides reliable information and reduces the time required for development. PMI defines a practice guide as a standards product that provides supporting supplemental information and instructions for the application of PMI standards. Practice guides are limited consensus-based standards and do not go through the public exposure draft process. However, practice guides may evolve into full consensus standards.

1

INTRODUCTION

1.1 Purpose of this Practice Guide

As stated in the preface, this practice guide describes the work of requirements management as historically defined by PMI. It identifies the tasks that are performed as well as the essential knowledge needed to perform requirements management effectively on programs and projects. This practice guide is applicable to most programs and projects, whether they are focused on products, services, or other results. The concepts and techniques described in this guide are implementation-independent and can be used to develop manual or automated solutions, using any type of life cycle approach.

The purpose of this practice guide is to discuss the elements and criticality of requirements development and management for project and program success as defined by PMI. This is accomplished by:

- Providing a practical discussion of the requirements management work,
- Defining "what is" the work of requirements management as it relates to programs and projects, by defining the tasks, knowledge, and skills that the requirements management process comprises,
- Discussing why the work is important,
- Providing a description of the activities performed, and
- Explaining how different types of project life cycles impact the timing and type of requirements management work performed.

This guide is intended to be a stand-alone document and thus acts as a bridge between two important PMI documents: *A Guide to the Project Management Body of Knowledge (PMBOK® Guide)* – Fifth Edition [1][1] and *Business Analysis for Practitioners: A Practice Guide* [2].

The *PMBOK® Guide* – Fifth Edition identifies the subset of the project management body of knowledge that is generally recognized as good practice for developing and managing requirements.

The *PMBOK® Guide* states, "The integrative nature of project and program management can be understood by thinking of other types of activities performed while completing a project. Examples of some activities performed by the project management team are to develop, review, analyze, and understand the scope of the project. This includes the project and product requirements, criteria, assumptions, constraints, and other influences related to a project, and how each will be managed or addressed within the project. Completion of the product scope is

---

[1] The numbers in brackets refer to the list of references at the end of this practice guide.

measured against the product requirements. The success of the project is directly influenced by active stakeholder involvement in the discovery and decomposition of needs into requirements and by the care taken in determining, documenting, and managing the requirements of the product, service, or result of the project. Requirements include conditions of capabilities that are to be met by the project or present in the product, service, or result to satisfy an agreement to other formally imposed specifications."

Business Analysis for Practitioners: A Practice Guide describes the work of business analysis, which includes requirements development and requirements management tasks, how these tasks can be practically applied on programs and projects, and the essential knowledge and skills needed to perform them.

This practice guide defines the common processes for the development and management of requirements on projects and programs, and therefore serves as the bridge between the *PMBOK® Guide* – Fifth Edition, which speaks to requirements development and management from a high-level awareness perspective, and *Business Analysis for Practitioners: A Practice Guide*, which describes requirements development and management at a detailed level. This practice guide offers the middle ground, so project and program managers, other interested project team members, and stakeholders can learn more about the requirements process than is covered by the *PMBOK® Guide* and gain an appreciation for and knowledge of the complexity of requirements development and management that is detailed in *Business Analysis for Practitioners: A Practice Guide.*

The relationship among these documents provides an integrated approach for developing and managing requirements on projects and programs from an awareness level to a detailed level.

1.2 The Need for this Guide

When properly implemented and supported, the critical competency of developing and managing requirements enables the organization to meet stakeholder expectations, improve project performance, meet expected organizational benefits, and achieve tangible business outcomes.

According to PMI's annual *Pulse of the Profession®* research reports, poor requirements management is a major cause of project failure [3]. The *Pulse of the Profession®* research uncovered these related findings for organizations:

- Only 49% of respondents have the resources in place to perform requirements management properly.
- Only 33% of the respondents state that their leadership values requirements management as a critical competency for projects and strategic initiatives.
- Approximately 53% of respondents fail to use a formal process to validate requirements in an unbiased way.

The research emphasizes that organizations continue to experience project issues associated with poor performance of requirements-related activities.

1.3 Intended Audience for this Guide

This practice guide is intended for program and project managers who are ultimately responsible for the integration of the requirements development and management activities within the overall project effort and who need to understand the risks and impacts that poor requirements management is having on their projects and programs and need to receive guidance to address these deficiencies.

This document will also be valuable to anyone who is responsible for performing requirements work, or for project stakeholders who interact with practitioners performing requirements activities. It was also developed to help those interested in improving their requirements-related competencies and for those interested in improving their knowledge of requirements processes and the application of this work on programs and projects.

1.4 Summary

The principles of requirements development and management as described in this practice guide should be appropriately applied based on the specifics of a project and the organizational environment. Effective requirements practices provide organizational benefits when they are consistent with organizational strategy and objectives by implementing good practice principles aligned with strong organizational commitment.

2

REQUIREMENTS MANAGEMENT OVERVIEW

To describe the relationship between requirements management and project management, an understanding of the definitions of a project, a requirement, and project management is needed. *A Guide to the Project Management Body of Knowledge (PMBOK® Guide) – Fifth Edition* defines these terms as follows:

- **Project**. A temporary endeavor undertaken to create a unique product, service, or result.
- **Requirement**. A condition or capability that is required to be present in a product, service, or result to satisfy a contract or other formally imposed specification.
- **Project management**. The application of knowledge, skills, tools, and techniques to project activities to meet the project requirements.

Project management is an integrative and iterative undertaking, meaning that actions taken during one process typically affect other related processes. Requirements development and requirements management are also integrative and iterative undertakings. PMI's definition of requirements management includes both requirements development and requirements management activities, so a definition of each term is provided to help solidify this understanding.

Requirements management encompasses the tasks of establishing a requirements baseline and maintaining traceability, change control, and configuration management.

Requirements development encompasses the tasks of eliciting and identifying requirements planning, analysis, documenting or specifying requirements, and validating and verifying requirements.

This section presents the following:

- Requirements management process overview,
- Interactions with *PMBOK® Guide* Process Groups,
- Interactions with *PMBOK® Guide* Knowledge Areas,
- Requirements management process considerations, and
- Requirements management associated communities of practice (described in Appendix X3).

2.1 Requirements Process Overview

The requirements process includes a common set of standardized and structured activities for developing and managing requirements on a project. While presented in sequence, each set of activities may occur independently or iteratively as program and project needs dictate. Each set of activities is described in more detail in subsequent sections, as follows:

- **Needs assessment** (Section 3). Needs assessments are conducted to identify and define a current business problem or opportunity at the portfolio level, typically pre-program and pre-project; however, during the course of a program or project, should external factors that influence or impact the program or project change, the needs assessment should be revisited to ensure previously made decisions remain valid. Section 3 discusses the process and considerations for needs assessments.

- **Requirements management planning** (Section 4). In conjunction with the development of a program or project management plan, the requirements management plan or business analysis plan is a critical portion of the overall project planning activities. Planning the requirements activities ensures the optimal requirements approach is pursued for the program or project.

- **Requirements elicitation** (Section 5). In this domain, the team elicits the necessary information to develop the solution requirements. Elicitation is the activity of drawing out information from stakeholders and other sources to further understand the needs of the business, in order to address a problem or opportunity and identify the stakeholders' preferences and conditions for the solution that will address those needs.

- **Requirements analysis** (Section 6). This domain focuses on examining, decomposing, and synthesizing the elicited information into an actionable set of requirements that fulfill the stated goals and objectives.

- **Requirements monitoring and controlling** (Section 7). Requirements are continually traced, monitored, and controlled to ensure the product scope is continually managed throughout the project and changes to the requirements are placed in scope only when approved.

- **Solution evaluation** (Section 8). Solution evaluation is concerned with the activities performed to validate a solution that is about to be or that has already been implemented.

- **Project or phase closure** (Section 9). Upon program or project closure, the product, service, or result has been transitioned from a development state to a maintenance state. Solution evaluation activities are performed on an as-needed basis to ensure the solution continues to meet the needs of the business and continues to deliver the expected value.

Figure 2-1 shows the flow of information during the requirements process across programs and projects. The process may be iterated as necessary.

2.1.1 Requirements Management and Change

As depicted in Figure 2-1, the requirements process is iterative. A key principle of program and project management is that progressive elaboration will lead to change. The *PMBOK® Guide* defines progressive elaboration as "the iterative process of increasing the level of detail in a project management plan as greater amounts of information and more accurate estimates become available." This concept relates directly to requirements development and management. At the onset of a requirements process, a given set of information is known. As requirements are elicited for the product, service, or result, more is known and original assumptions may change based on this new knowledge. As more information is discovered, each step in the requirements process supports change and adapts to it.

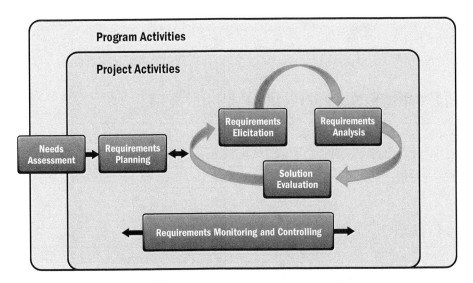

Figure 2-1. Requirements Process Diagram

2.2 Interaction with *PMBOK® Guide* Process Groups

This section discusses the mapping of the requirements process to the Project Management Process Groups (as depicted in Figure 2-2). The management and development of requirements can be managed as an overall program, a distinct project, or as part of a project for a given product, service, or result. Figure 2-2 represents the

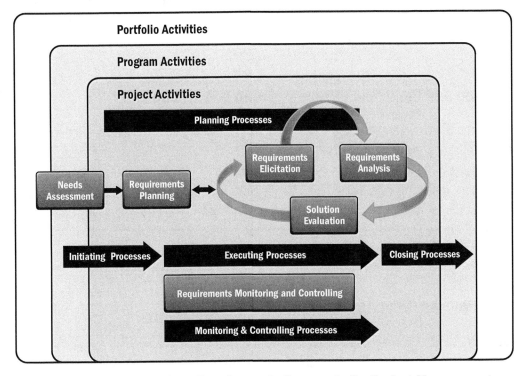

Figure 2-2. Mapping of the Requirements Process to the Project Management Process Groups

relationship of the requirements process to the project management processes. The activities shown in Figure 2-2 may be iterative.

2.2.1 Initiating Process Group Interactions

The Initiating Process Group consists of those activities performed to define a new project or new phase of an existing project by obtaining authorization to start the project or phase. The outputs of the initiating phase inform the Planning Process Group.

2.2.2 Planning Process Group Interactions

The Planning Process Group consists of those tasks required to establish the scope of the project, refine the objectives, and define the course of action required to attain the objectives that the project was undertaken to achieve. The planning processes in the Project Scope Management Knowledge Area are performed to achieve those objectives. Those processes include Plan Scope Management, Define Scope, Collect Requirements, and Create WBS.

2.2.3 Executing Process Group Interactions

The Executing Process Group consists of those tasks performed to complete the work defined in the project management plan to satisfy the program and project specifications. In the context of the requirements process, activities include: eliciting the requirements (Section 5), analyzing the requirements (Section 6), documenting the requirements, and validating and verifying the requirements and solution (Section 8).

2.2.4 Monitoring and Controlling Process Group Interactions

The project scope is the work performed to deliver a product, service, or result. The product scope comprises the features and functions that characterize the product, service, or result. Requirements describe features and functions for the project; therefore, there is a direct relationship between the number of requirements and the product scope, which impacts the project scope. The requirements baseline is the boundary that contains all the approved requirements for the project, project phase, iteration, increment, release, or any other part of a project. The Monitoring and Controlling Process Group consists of the tasks completed to ensure that requirements are approved and managed throughout the project life cycle as described in Section 7.

2.2.5 Closing Process Group Interactions

The Closing Process Group consists of those tasks performed to finalize all activities across all Process Groups to formally close the project or phase. Closing activities are performed at the project level and include documenting lessons learned; providing knowledge transfer; reviewing completed or remaining artifacts; transitioning the product, service, or result to operations; or performing other benefits-sustaining activities (Section 9).

Within the Closing Process Group are the requirements-related activities of assisting with the transition of the solution from development to production, conducting lessons learned to capture relevant lessons concerning the requirements process, and ensuring the solution is evaluated on an ongoing basis, as defined by the business, to ensure value continues to be delivered by the new solution.

2.3 Interactions with *PMBOK® Guide* Knowledge Areas

The requirements process is influenced by and has interactions with many of the *PMBOK® Guide* Knowledge Areas. It should be noted that the life cycles and related activities involved in the development and management of requirements are distinct from the project management life cycle. The primary domains for requirements management are described in Sections 2.3.1 through 2.3.2. In addition, Section 2.3.3 discusses interactions with other Knowledge Areas in the *PMBOK® Guide*.

2.3.1 Requirements and Stakeholder Management

Project Stakeholder Management includes the tasks required to identify all people or organizations impacted by the project, to analyze stakeholder characteristics for impact on the project or program, and to develop appropriate management strategies for effectively engaging stakeholders in decisions and execution. Stakeholder involvement and buy-in are also essential for the success of the requirements process. Proactively and methodically managing stakeholder needs and expectations helps to facilitate a successful outcome.

2.3.2 Requirements and Communications Management

Project Communications Management includes the tasks required to ensure timely and appropriate planning, collection, creation, distribution, storage, retrieval, management, controlling, monitoring, and the ultimate disposition of project information. Project managers spend most of their time communicating with team members and other stakeholders regardless of whether they are internal or external to the organization.

Communication is also an important factor in the requirements process. The information used across requirement activities is based on input from stakeholders and dependent on timely communications to both the internal team and the cross-section of stakeholders.

2.3.3 Requirements and Other Knowledge Areas

The resulting requirements baseline impacts other *PMBOK® Guide* Knowledge Areas: Project Integration Management, Project Time Management, Project Cost Management, Project Quality Management, Project Human Resource Management, Project Risk Management, and Project Procurement Management. These Knowledge Areas will influence and be influenced by the requirements process. It is incumbent upon the person with responsibility for requirements to be aware of the potential impacts to these Knowledge Areas and provide timely related communications to the project manager or appropriate stakeholders.

2.4 Project Life Cycle Considerations

The *PMBOK® Guide* (Section 5.2) states that project life cycles occupy a continuum from predictive to adaptive. It is essential that the chosen requirements approach aligns with the selected project life cycle and the project characteristics such as complexity and risk level and team distribution. Factors that characterize the positions of life cycles for projects within the continuum include, but are not limited to, the various ways requirements and plans are handled; how risk, schedule, resources, and cost are managed; and the timing and level of involvement of key stakeholders. The continuum of life cycles for projects is illustrated in Figure 2-3.

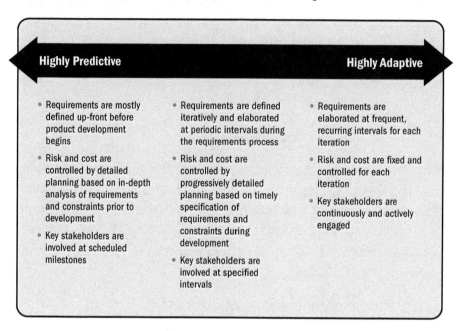

Highly Predictive

Highly Adaptive

- Requirements are mostly defined up-front before product development begins

- Risk and cost are controlled by detailed planning based on in-depth analysis of requirements and constraints prior to development

- Key stakeholders are involved at scheduled milestones

- Requirements are defined iteratively and elaborated at periodic intervals during the requirements process

- Risk and cost are controlled by progressively detailed planning based on timely specification of requirements and constraints during development

- Key stakeholders are involved at specified intervals

- Requirements are elaborated at frequent, recurring intervals for each iteration

- Risk and cost are fixed and controlled for each iteration

- Key stakeholders are continuously and actively engaged

Figure 2-3. The Continuum of Project Life Cycles

The importance of the project life cycle to the requirements process is best demonstrated by understanding how different project life cycles impact the requirements-related work. For example, highly predictive project life cycles are characterized by ensuring all requirements elicitation and analysis work is completed before the start of any solution design and development work. One cycle of requirements analysis is performed and, upon requirements approval, requirements are baselined and a formal change control process enacted. The objective is to use formal processes and detailed documentation to control requirements and manage change across the project.

With adaptive life cycles, the requirements process is much less an "all or nothing" approach. Instead, requirements are elicited throughout the project, which provides more opportunity for the business to progressively elaborate its needs as more information and understanding about the solution is acquired. Adaptive life cycles impact the requirements process by supporting an iterative approach to requirements elicitation and analysis, higher stakeholder collaboration, and progressive planning. Much less emphasis is placed on documentation because the requirements are evolving. Any emphasis on heavy documentation would be wasted in such a dynamic environment.

The same requirements-related activities are performed in either life cycle. It is the timing of the work and the level of thoroughness and formality of the documentation that distinguishes the different requirements processes across life cycles. It is for these reasons that the selected project life cycle is an important factor when planning the requirements-related work.

2

3

NEEDS ASSESSMENT

Needs assessment begins before the project life cycle and analyzes requirements for a business problem or strategic organizational need. As depicted in Figure 3-1, requirements that are initiated at the portfolio, program, and/or project level are synchronized throughout the life cycle into a product, service, or result that is intended to meet those requirements and provide business value.

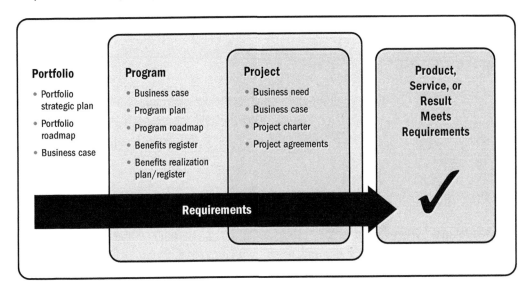

Figure 3-1. Requirements Cross All Levels to Provide Business Value

The key benefit of performing a needs assessment is the creation of a high-level needs definition that will ultimately be used to determine viable solution options that drive the development of a business case and subsequent requirements. The business need is assessed to understand the goals and objectives of the organization, define problems and opportunities, assess the current capabilities of an organization, define the desired future state, and identify capability gaps.

3.1 Needs Assessment Results

The result of maximizing the effectiveness of the needs assessment process will increase the likelihood of requirements being implemented successfully within the product, service, or result as documented. It is critical that the results of the needs assessment be understood before initiating the program or project. The results of the needs assessment define the problem to be solved or the opportunity to be exploited, and provide the basis from which the remainder of the requirements process is performed. It is also critical that the requirements support the strategic objectives and align to the organizational strategy described in the business case.

3.2 Needs Assessment Portfolio-Level Activities

This section provides an overview of the activities performed to define requirements when the project is part of a portfolio.

In the Portfolio Strategic Management Knowledge Area, there are two portfolio management processes that help to define requirements: Develop Portfolio Strategic Plan and Define Portfolio Roadmap.

3.2.1 Develop Portfolio Strategic Plan

The portfolio strategic plan conveys the alignment of the portfolio's individual components to the organizational strategy, future benefit, and stakeholder expectations. The portfolio strategic plan conveys the key strategic assumptions, constraints, dependencies, and priorities that influence the requirements.

3.2.2 Define Portfolio Roadmap

The portfolio roadmap provides insight to the strategic prioritization mapping of the portfolio and its components. The roadmap is the initial basis upon which dependencies between initiatives and deliverables are established. The roadmap should provide the context for requirements efforts on the project.

3.3 Needs Assessment Program-Level Activities

This section provides an overview of the activities performed to define requirements when the project is part of a program.

3.3.1 Define Business Case or Equivalent

The program business case provides insight into alternative solution options, time to market, constraints, and philosophy behind the business need. It also contains a clear vision statement for the initiative, identifies an initial set of known stakeholders and their needs, and identifies any constraints or dependencies. Requirements definition is enhanced by understanding the alternative solution options, expected benefits, and other program requirements to improve the success of the program and component projects.

3.3.2 Develop Program Plan

The program plan and other high-level plans required by a customer or internal processes assist the component projects with detailed planning. The program planning process is highly iterative and may involve coordination between the project manager and the program manager to develop. During program planning, external influences, organizational constraints, and business strategies influence the requirements outlined in the program plan.

3.3.3 Develop Program Roadmap

The program roadmap provides the high-level timeline, benefits, and strategy that the project is expected to accomplish. Major milestones from the component projects are typically included in the program roadmap. Requirements are monitored to ensure they continue to address the needs of the program and/or portfolio.

3.3.4 Create Benefits Register

The benefits register collects and lists the planned benefits for the program; it is used to measure and communicate the delivery of benefits throughout the life of the program. It defines the appropriate performance measures for each of the benefits. The benefits register typically includes the person, group, or organization responsible for delivering each of the benefits.

3.3.5 Engage Stakeholders

Stakeholder engagement is the work involved to maintain stakeholder involvement across the initiative. Stakeholder engagement begins with the process of identifying the people, groups, or organizations that may affect, be affected by, or have an interest in a decision, activity, or outcome of a program or project. A stakeholder analysis is conducted to identify and understand the needs of the stakeholders. Stakeholder preferences, characteristics, and expectations influence requirements-planning decisions.

3.3.6 Develop Benefits Realization Plan

The benefits realization plan defines when a benefit is delivered by a program or project. This plan defines the benefits, how they are achieved, and how the benefits link to constituent project outputs like the work performed in solution evaluation. There are defined metrics and procedures to measure the benefits, to describe how the resulting capability is transitioned to an operational state, and to describe how the organization can sustain the benefits. Please consult Appendix X5 of *The Standard for Program Management* – Third Edition [4] or Section 6 of *The Standard for Portfolio Management* – Third Edition [5] for additional information.

3.4 Needs Assessment Project-Level Activities

This section provides an overview of initiating the requirements process for the product, service, or result.

3.4.1 Develop Business Case

A business case (or equivalent) is normally developed before project initiation. The needs assessment and business case build the foundation for determining the project objectives and serve as inputs to a project charter. The business case defines the strategic need, objectives, and recommended solution options. The business need provides the perspective as to why the organization needs the project.

3.4.2 Document and Communicate Results

The business case should align with the portfolio strategic plan and program plan, and thus should be communicated with the sponsor and other appropriate stakeholders.

3.5 Needs Assessment Techniques

Sections 3.5.1 through 3.5.4 describe common techniques used during needs assessment.

3.5.1 SWOT Analysis

An analysis of strengths, weaknesses, opportunities, and threats (SWOT analysis) is a widely used technique to help understand high-level views surrounding a business need and to compare options at any level of project management. The SWOT analysis becomes more detailed at the project level and more strategic at the portfolio or program level, and may be used to understand the strengths and weaknesses (focused inwardly or internally) and opportunities and threats (focused outwardly or externally) of the organization. A SWOT analysis may help the organization mitigate a problem. For additional information, refer to Section 11.2.2.6 of the *PMBOK® Guide* – Fifth Edition or Section 2.4.2 of *Business Analysis for Practitioners: A Practice Guide*.

3.5.2 Decision Analysis

Decision analysis is a group of techniques that provide a basis for structured, analytical decision making. For example, decision trees and decision tables depict a series of decisions and their outcomes. Decision trees work best with binary choices (i.e., yes or no), and decision tables can be used when more choices exist and the analysis is becoming complex. For more information, refer to Section 4.10.9.2 of *Business Analysis for Practitioners: A Practice Guide*.

3.5.3 Gap Analysis

Gap analysis is a technique used to compare the current assessment of organizational capability against a future desired state. The result is normally referred to as the "to be state" of a solution (see Section 2.4.7 of *Business Analysis for Practitioners: A Practice Guide*).

3.5.4 Benchmarking

Benchmarking, like competitive analysis, provides insights into how other organizations are responding to the same challenges experienced by the performing organization. Benchmarking is used to compare an organization's actual or planned practices, such as processes and operations, to those of comparable organizations to identify best practices, generate ideas for improvement, and provide a basis for measuring performance.

3

REQUIREMENTS MANAGEMENT PLANNING

Requirements management planning activities occur within the Planning Process Group. The key benefit of this domain is that it provides guidance and direction on how requirements will be developed and managed throughout the project. The plan is developed, reviewed, and updated to reflect the specific activities of the life cycle domains from elicitation, analysis, monitoring, and controlling through solution evaluation. The success factors, planning activities, and tools and techniques are described in Sections 4.1 through 4.3.

4.1 Requirements Management Planning Success Factors

The success factors outlined in Sections 4.1.1 through 4.1.4 are considered vital to maximize the effectiveness of the requirements planning process and increase the likelihood of project success.

4.1.1 Organizational Commitment

Organizational commitment is paramount to the success of any strategic work. The requirements process should be aligned with the organization's goals and values, and a sponsor should be engaged. PMI's annual *Pulse of the Profession*® [3] research report indicates lack of sponsorship support as a leading contributor to project failure. Therefore, sponsor and stakeholder commitment to the requirements process is paramount during requirements planning.

4.1.2 Recognizing the Value of Requirements Management Planning

Requirements management planning should be recognized as a valuable domain that provides a positive potential return on investment for organizational management, stakeholders (both internal and external), project managers, and team members.

4.1.3 Stakeholder Engagement and Collaboration

Stakeholders should be engaged early and often throughout the life cycle. Stakeholder analysis is often conducted during the planning domain so the project team can understand the stakeholder impacts and influences on the requirements process as early as possible. This analysis is performed iteratively and is revisited throughout the project as new stakeholders are discovered or existing stakeholders are determined to no longer be impacted by the proposed solution. Lack of stakeholder analysis and engagement may lead to incomplete, incorrect, or missed requirements.

4.1.4 Integration with Project Management Activities

Requirements development and management do not exist in isolation from other project management processes. A successful requirements plan requires integrated execution with the project management plan.

4.2 Requirements Management Planning Activities

Sections 4.2.1 through 4.2.4 cover the four core processes of requirements management planning.

4.2.1 Stakeholder Analysis and Engagement

Stakeholder analysis and engagement is critical to the success of the requirements management plan. Stakeholder analysis and identification is the process of analyzing and identifying the people, groups, or organizations that may affect, be affected by, or have an interest in a decision, activity, or outcome of a program or project. Stakeholders may be internal or external to the organization. Further stakeholder identification is conducted during requirements planning activities to set expectations with the key stakeholders to ensure they understand the requirements activities that will be performed and to gain their buy-in and support for the requirements process before work begins. Stakeholder preferences, characteristics, and expectations influence requirements management planning decisions. The steps involved in the stakeholder analysis are described in Sections 4.2.1.1 through 4.2.1.3.

4.2.1.1 Generate or Refine the Stakeholder Register

An initial stakeholder register may have been developed as a part of the needs assessment, or the work to produce the project management plan, stakeholder management plan, communications plan, or other plan documents. Whether there is a need to start anew or begin with an existing register of stakeholders, this step analyzes and identifies the stakeholders who will have a role in the requirements process. The register may include stakeholders such as those who will:

- Provide sponsorship for the project;
- Benefit from the project outcomes;
- Be responsible for the project outcomes;
- Define the product service or result;
- Provide support;
- Articulate the benefits;
- Provide financial backing;
- Use the solution; and
- Implement the solution.

After the register is generated and reviewed, the stakeholders are characterized and grouped.

4.2.1.2 Group and Characterize Stakeholders

Once the stakeholder register is complete, an analysis of the characteristics of the identified stakeholders should be performed. Some commonly applied characteristics for consideration are attitude, complexity, culture, experience, level of influence, location, and availability. Brief descriptions of these are in Section 3.3.2 of *Business Analysis for Practitioners: A Practice Guide*.

Once characteristics are understood, stakeholders can be grouped. Groupings can be structured by similar interests, common needs, level of importance, etc., but are used to help identify unique groups for eliciting requirements.

It is important to make sure that there are clear roles, responsibilities, and accountabilities; therefore, a single primary contact should be identified for each task. A commonly used approach to organizing these assignments, known as either RACI or ACRI, characterizes and groups stakeholders into one or more of four categories:

- **Responsible.** Person(s) performing the work.
- **Accountable.** Person(s) approving the work or assigning a delegate to approve for them.
- **Consulted.** Person or group (often subject matter experts) to be consulted for input.
- **Informed.** Person or group to be apprised of progress.

Once the stakeholder register is reviewed and approved, the information collected in this step can be later documented in the requirements management plan. As stakeholders change over the course of the project, the register is updated to reflect the current stakeholders.

4.2.1.3 Manage Stakeholder Engagement

Through proactive communication and working directly with stakeholders to meet the project objectives, stakeholders are engaged and managed throughout the requirements life cycle process. It is important to understand their needs and expectations, address issues as they arise, and foster the appropriate engagement throughout the life cycle in order to gain increased support and reduced resistance, significantly increasing the chance to achieve project success.

For additional information on Project Stakeholder Management, please refer to Section 13 of the *PMBOK® Guide* and Section 3.3 of *Business Analysis for Practitioners: A Practice Guide*.

4.2.2 Requirements Management Planning Initiation

Generally, there is a list of project artifacts that describe the project. It is essential at the start of the requirements process to clearly understand the initial project scope statement and project objectives. The key tasks for initiating requirements management planning are described in Sections 4.2.2.1 and 4.2.2.2.

4.2.2.1 Gather Project Information

In the project management plan, the scope statement describes the scope, major deliverables, assumptions, and constraints for the project. Leveraging this foundational information is an appropriate starting point, as the work within a project should link back to this scope statement. To better understand the enterprise environmental information in which the project is being performed, additional information can be leveraged to provide the context for the scope statement which may include (but is not limited to):

- Organizational strategic plans,
- Feasibility studies,
- Needs assessment(s),
- Business case(s),
- Concept of operations documents,
- Program management plan (when applicable),
- Project charter,
- Project management plan,
- Project scope statement,
- Contractual documents, and
- Customer specifications.

By reviewing the appropriate associated documents, the context and enterprise environmental factors can be better understood, leading to the development of an effective requirements plan.

4.2.2.2 Identify Organizational Standards and Guidance

Many organizations have established operating procedures, standards, and predeveloped tools, templates, techniques, and process documents. It is important to investigate the existence of organizational standards or guidance that impact the requirements process up front. This can save considerable time by not having to develop processes, protocols, templates, etc., that are already in place. In addition, when existing processes are not followed, significant rework may be incurred.

For organizations that do not have organizational standards and guidance in place, there are numerous resources available, such as standards development organizations (e.g., PMI), consulting firms, and Internet resources. As processes are introduced and improved, it is a good practice to build a process library to institutionalize standards and guidance.

4.2.3 Develop the Requirements Management Plan

The requirements management plan is a component of the project management plan and describes how the requirement activities of the project will be planned and managed. The project life cycle (predictive to adaptive) strongly influences how requirements are planned, developed, and managed.

4.2.3.1 Core Components of the Requirements Management Plan

The requirements management plan focuses on the scope of requirements activities to be conducted and deliverables to be produced. The core components of the requirements management plan can include, but are not limited to:

- How requirements should developed, tracked, managed, validated, and reported;
- What the roles and responsibilities are for those participating in requirements activities;
- What the authorization and key decision-making process is;
- How requirements should be prioritized, approved, and maintained;
- How the acceptance criteria are determined for the requirements and solution;
- What product metrics are used and the rationale for using them;
- What the traceability structure is and the implementation to reflect which requirement attributes will be captured on the traceability matrix; and
- How requirements will be documented and communicated to stakeholders.

In addition, information pertinent to planning, such as the list of involved stakeholders and the roles they will fulfill during the requirements process, may be included as part of this document or as a part of the overall project management plan.

A requirements management plan has evolved in some organizations to also encompass planning decisions for business analysis. Section 3.4 of *Business Analysis for Practitioners: A Practice Guide* discusses the relationship between a requirements management plan and a business analysis plan.

4.2.4 Launch the Requirements Management Plan

Once the requirements management plan is complete, it should be reviewed with key stakeholders to reduce the risk of stakeholders failing to support the work to be performed. Once reviewed, it is presented to the sponsor and stakeholders for approval. Approval may be formal and require a signature or may be informal and only require verbal acceptance. There may be an organizational or project life cycle process that defines how approval should be attained. Once approved, the plan may be updated throughout the requirements process.

4.3 Requirements Tools

During the planning process, any requirements tools in use by the organization should be identified and then determined when and how they will be used.

5

REQUIREMENTS ELICITATION

The purpose of this section is to expand upon the Collect Requirements process described in the *PMBOK® Guide* and align it to Section 4 of *Business Analysis for Practitioners: A Practice Guide*.

Elicitation is a discovery process used to bring forward or produce information relevant to the project or program by drawing out information from stakeholders and other sources. This process aims to identify the causes of the business problem or the reasons for addressing an opportunity, as well as the information to be used to derive a sufficient level of requirements to enable a solution to be developed and implemented.

The elicitation domain uses progressive elaboration, as all requirements are generally not known or revealed at the onset of a project or program. Elicitation is largely conducted in an iterative, ongoing manner. As details emerge over the project life cycle, requirements are likely to be further decomposed, and new information will be translated into additional requirements. Requirements may also surface as analysis and other activities within the requirements process are performed.

In an adaptive life cycle, elicitation and analysis are performed throughout the project as part of defining the initial product backlog and grooming the backlog as details are analyzed and features are implemented for each iteration.

This section outlines generally accepted activities used to successfully identify and capture requirements, as well as key factors to consider when determining the appropriate elicitation techniques for a particular project life cycle or approach. The major components of this domain are outlined in Sections 5.1 through 5.3.

5.1 Requirements Elicitation Success Factors

A range of factors is considered vital to maximize the effectiveness of requirements elicitation and reduce the likelihood of having incomplete, inaccurate, or missing requirements.

5.1.1 Planning and Preparation

Some elicitation planning occurred during the requirements management plan process. Within requirements elicitation, planning focuses on how to conduct elicitation sessions, which stakeholders to involve, and in which order. Preparation should be completed before requirements can be properly elicited. This initial planning is used to assess the level of effort required to elicit requirements for the project, and to plan the elicitation tasks that will be performed. The size, complexity, and type of project should be considered, as the elicitation activities will vary based on these characteristics.

5.1.2 Active Stakeholder Engagement

Stakeholders are a principal source of requirements, which places them at the center of many project and program issues related to unrealistic expectations, lack of user involvement, and ambiguous, unclear requirements. For this reason, active support and participation of key stakeholders should be fostered and maintained throughout the elicitation process. Input should be collected from a broad, diverse set of stakeholders to confirm that varying perspectives are captured and to reduce the risk of missing requirements.

5.1.3 Defined Business/Organizational Need

A properly conducted needs assessment lays the foundation for achieving the goals and objectives of the business or organization. A comprehensive understanding of the business need, problem, or opportunity helps to determine that the right information is elicited and the appropriate stakeholders and elicitation techniques to obtain that information are selected.

5.1.4 Domain Knowledge

The person responsible for elicitation should be competent in the domain or have access to subject matter experts for support so as to ask the right questions during elicitation activities. Understanding the relevant terms, processes, and procedures within a specified domain greatly increases the ability to accurately define and examine requirements.

5.2 Requirements Elicitation Activities

At this point, eliciting requirements for the solution is performed to address the defined problem/opportunity. Elicitation involves the discovery and translation of needs into requirements and includes the following activities: selecting the appropriate elicitation techniques, conducting the actual elicitation, and documenting the outputs.

5.2.1 Plan for Elicitation

Before the actual elicitation, more detailed preparation is required such as drafting agendas, scheduling conferences for elicitation workshops, inviting stakeholders, etc.

Careful consideration should be given to the following elements:

- **Activities.** Even though activities were previously defined in Requirements Management Planning, now that more is known about the problem/opportunity to be solved or addressed and the stakeholders involved, the techniques to be used are revisited. Generally, a combination of techniques is employed depending upon the organizational culture, schedule constraints, and relevant knowledge and skills of the person responsible for eliciting requirements.

- **Requirements sources.** Determine the potential sources of information that are needed to develop requirements. These sources can be internal or external to the organization and include specific people, reference material, or other documentation relevant to the project or program scope. This information may exist in many forms, including user manuals, procedures, market research, or governmental regulations. Existing requirements can also be viable sources of information. Those requirements that are common across projects and programs should be considered for reuse to improve productivity of the elicitation effort.

- **Resources.** Identify the project resources that are required to participate in the elicitation activities. These resources may include stakeholders, equipment, and facilities.

- **Expected deliverables.** While typically addressed during Requirements Management Planning, revisit the deliverables or work products that will be created during the elicitation process, because more is now known about the problem/opportunity to be solved or addressed. Deliverables will vary depending on the project life cycle and chosen elicitation technique(s). More predictive life cycles typically require formal requirements specifications, whereas highly adaptive life cycles focus on more lightweight documentation, such as user stories.

5.2.2 Define Types of Requirements

Requirements can be classified into various categories to provide clarity and context to the issue.

These categories also help define what information needs to be elicited and the source of that information. Expert judgment, standards, or common practices associated with an organization, industry, or community of knowledge may be used to determine the types of requirements and level of detail sufficient to develop the solution.

Common classifications include:

- **Business requirements.** Describe the high-level needs of the overall organization to address a problem or opportunity. These requirements provide the rationale for why a project or program is launched.

- **Stakeholder requirements.** Express the needs of a specific stakeholder or group of stakeholders, which may include customers, users, or suppliers. These requirements communicate the material interest of the stakeholders in the outcome of the product, service, or result. These requirements provide a basis for identifying the solution requirements.

- **Solution requirements.** Describe the features and functions that the product, service, or result needs to exhibit to satisfy the business and stakeholder requirements. Solution requirements may include requirements related to technology and standard compliance. These are often grouped into two categories: functional and nonfunctional requirements.

  - *Functional requirements* denote particular behaviors and operations that the solution will perform. These focus on the required functionality to enable stakeholders to accomplish their objectives, which in turn fulfills the business need.

  - *Nonfunctional requirements* describe certain environmental conditions or required attributes to ensure the product or service operates effectively.

- **Transition requirements.** Describe the temporary capabilities that are essential to migrate from the current state to a future state environment. Requirements that fall into this category include conversion of data from the current system and training needed to address skill gaps.

- **Project requirements.** Describe the actions, processes, and other conditions that the project needs to satisfy. These requirements focus on the execution of the work required to deliver the solution.

- **Quality requirements.** Describe the criteria needed to ensure completion of project deliverables and demonstrate compliance with identified standards and quality metrics.

- **Program requirements.** Describe the specifications and outcomes for successful implementation and delivery of the program benefits.

Project, quality, and program requirements are not a part of the requirements process but are a part of the project or program work. These requirements are typically the responsibility of the project or program manager but may be delegated as appropriate.

5.2.3 Conduct Elicitation Activities

Elicitation is an exploratory activity that draws out implicit and hidden information. During elicitation, input is received by consulting a broad range of stakeholders, as well as reviewing existing systems, historical records, and documentation. This ensures that varying viewpoints are represented and the project goals and objectives are well understood.

While elicitation is generally an iterative process for most projects, the timing and degree of iteration varies based on the project life cycle. In a plan-driven or predictive environment, elicitation activities are typically conducted as early as possible in the project. Even in a predictive life cycle, requirements are expected to evolve as the project progresses, both to include increasing levels of detail and to address changes. However, the elicitation of requirements should cease once the solution has been defined to a sufficient level so it can be built. For more adaptive life cycles, elicitation activities occur continuously throughout the project life cycle in conjunction with requirements analysis. The initial work is performed to define the vision, scope, and high-level business needs of the problem or opportunity. As the project evolves, the scope is further evaluated and decomposed into a set of requirements, also known as the product backlog, one iteration at a time. This just-in-time method allows the project team to focus on delivering a portion of the functionality and to receive feedback on the requirements before moving to the next iteration.

5.2.4 Document and Communicate Results

The outcome of elicitation activities should be recorded to properly examine and synthesize the relevant information during the analysis process. It is important that the documented results are consolidated, communicated with, and reviewed by the stakeholders to ensure accuracy. This information may be documented in a number of forms, including audio recordings, meeting minutes, interview notes, and survey responses. Work products can be described as informal documents or a collection of notes and diagrams created during elicitation.

These work products may or may not evolve into requirements. However, they are necessary throughout the elicitation process to clarify the information received and identify other items that require additional research or explanation. These additional items should be documented in the form of open issues or action items and recorded appropriately using an action item or issue-tracking mechanism.

5.3 Requirements Elicitation Techniques

A wide range of techniques is available for requirements elicitation, with each one having its own strengths and weaknesses. These techniques may be used alone or in combination with others to achieve the desired outcome. It is necessary to understand the characteristics of each technique before selecting and applying the appropriate ones to ensure an optimal exchange of information.

Some commonly used techniques are described in Sections 5.3.1 through 5.3.9.

5.3.1 Interviews

An interview is a methodical approach used to elicit information from stakeholders by asking relevant questions and documenting the responses. During this activity, questions are posed to program and project participants to identify functions and capabilities that should exist in the end product, service, or result. Interviews may be structured, where questions are prepared in advance of a meeting, or unstructured, where questions are asked in a free-flowing manner based on responses to previous questions.

5.3.2 Facilitated Workshops

Facilitated workshops convene stakeholders or multidisciplinary teams in a focused and structured session to identify requirements, reconcile differences, and reach consensus among the participants. These interactive workshops enable discovery of requirements while resolving conflicts early in the project life cycle.

5.3.3 Focus Groups

Focus groups assemble prequalified participants, such as subject matter experts, in a group setting to share their attitudes and expectations about a particular product, service, or result. The group members voice their opinions and provide clarity on specific topics. This technique provides qualitative feedback that can be further examined as requirements are analyzed.

5.3.4 Brainstorming

Brainstorming is a group technique used to generate multiple ideas related to a particular subject. It uses the collective input from the group to understand different perspectives of a problem or solution and to build upon each other's ideas. This method relies heavily on the contribution of its participants to gain valuable information regarding a specific topic. Other examples of group creativity techniques include use of the nominal group technique, idea/mind-mapping, affinity diagram, and multicriteria decision analysis.

5.3.5 Questionnaires and Surveys

Questionnaires and surveys are techniques used to quickly solicit and obtain information from a large number of users. These techniques involve prepared questions to elicit subjective and demographic data from respondents. The data is analyzed to extract relevant requirements or may be used to prepare for further elicitation. Questionnaires and surveys are most effective when quick responses are needed and stakeholders are geographically dispersed. Questionnaires and surveys can be closed-ended or open-ended. Closed-ended questions provide the respondent with a predefined list of responses from which to choose. In contrast, open-ended questions allow the respondent to answer questions in his or her own words.

5.3.6 Document Analysis

A substantial amount of information can be uncovered by reviewing and analyzing existing documentation. Document analysis inspects a wide range of materials, such as a glossary of terms, strategic and business plans, process flows, problem/issue logs, regulations, policies, and procedures to discover and/or verify requirements. This technique provides a good starting point for eliciting relevant product details. Using up-to-date and accurate documentation is important to safeguard against erroneous information.

5.3.7 Interface Analysis

Interface analysis is used to define requirements by examining system interactions between users, processes, and other system components. It helps to establish relationships and boundaries by determining the input and output needs of each interfacing system. This method is useful for identifying additional stakeholders who may be impacted by changes to the system interfaces, as well as potential interoperability issues.

5.3.8 Prototypes

Prototyping is a method of obtaining early feedback on requirements by providing a working model of the expected product before actual development. This model is used to progressively refine requirements by giving stakeholders an opportunity to test, experiment, and provide feedback. Prototyping is performed in an iterative manner that consists of prototype creation, evaluation, and revision. It continues until the requirements obtained from the prototype are sufficiently complete to move forward in the requirements process. In an adaptive environment, prototyping is considered to be an evolutionary development process that transforms the requirements into a subset of functionality that provides value.

5.3.9 Observation

Observation, also known as "job shadowing," provides a direct way of viewing people in their environment to see how they perform their jobs or tasks and carry out processes within their environment. This technique is particularly helpful for eliciting tacit requirements that are difficult to verbalize.

5

REQUIREMENTS ANALYSIS

Analysis is the process used to examine, decompose, and synthesize information to further understand it and the features and capabilities of the solution. Throughout the analysis domain, requirements are captured in various formats and decomposed to obtain the necessary level of detail.

Similar to elicitation, analysis is performed using a progressive and iterative approach to examine the information to lower levels of detail to develop a set of requirements. The iteration and analysis continues until a sufficient level of requirements needed to formulate the solution is obtained.

In an adaptive life cycle, elicitation and analysis occur throughout the project or program as part of defining the initial backlog, grooming the backlog to refine requirements, and analyzing details for each iteration.

This section describes the processes recognized as good practices in requirements analysis, including success factors, activities, and techniques.

6.1 Requirements Analysis Success Factors

Achieving the objectives of requirements analysis is dependent on numerous factors as described in Sections 6.1.1 through 6.1.3.

6.1.1 Skilled Resources

Having the correct talent is vital to conducting meaningful analysis. Once the process has started, there is little opportunity to train and acquire the right skill set to effectively perform analysis.

6.1.2 Communication

Throughout analysis, frequent and timely communication with the project team, stakeholders, etc., is key to improving the quality of the requirements. This communication helps to further clarify uncertainties and avoid costly rework in downstream domains.

6.1.3 Collaboration

The success of analysis greatly depends on establishing a collaborative working relationship between the stakeholders involved in the requirements effort and the person performing the analysis. This environment enables open and effective communication that may foster the discovery of stakeholder expectations that should be vetted during the refinement of the requirements.

6.2 Requirements Analysis Activities

Analysis plays a critical role in confirming that the requirements are complete, accurate, and aligned with the business goals and objectives. In practice, analysis is performed using the outputs from requirements elicitation and includes planning, analyzing, and documenting results.

6.2.1 Plan for Analysis

It is essential to establish a strategy for how analysis will be performed. This strategy includes determining what activities and techniques will be used to yield the greatest benefit based on what is known about the project or program. Analysis planning also involves defining which tools to apply and how the outputs will be documented. The activities and techniques executed during this requirements analysis are governed by the requirements management plan. However, activities may be refined and adjusted as more details are discovered throughout the project.

Planning for effective requirements analysis also relies on careful review and consideration of additional factors (see Section 6.2.1.1).

6.2.1.1 Activities

Evaluate what types of analyses will be performed and identify the appropriate analysis techniques and tools to employ. Visual models, for example, provide context to better understand and clearly convey information. It is important to identify existing models in the organization to leverage as a starting point for analysis.

6.2.2 Conduct Analysis Activities

Requirements analysis is more than analyzing information to further understand it, complete it, and improve it. It involves structuring requirements in different views to capture varying perspectives, evaluating requirements for certain attributes, and integrating the collective information into written documentation. Requirements analysis is a continuous process. Conducting analysis includes six main components, which are described in Sections 6.2.2.1 through 6.2.2.6.

6.2.2.1 Identify, Analyze, and Document Requirements Attributes

Requirements attributes are specific characteristics or traits that capture key information about a requirement, such as the source, owner priority, complexity, rationale, and status. Requirements attributes are elicited as requirements are elicited. This information is used to aid in requirements traceability and monitoring throughout the project life cycle. Specifying attributes is critical to the analysis process as the information can be filtered, sorted, and validated to reveal discrepancies that may require additional analysis.

6.2.2.2 Select the Requirements Models

A component of analysis is the development of graphical or text models, which are helpful in finding gaps in information and identifying extraneous information. Requirements are modeled and refined to provide greater insight and correctness and to elicit additional information to define the details necessary to build the product, service, or result.

As some models are better suited for certain environments, it is important to select requirements models based on specific characteristics, type of project, methodology, timing, purpose, and level of abstraction.

Requirements models are constructed at various levels of detail. There are a number of categories and modeling notations available to assist in model development, which is described in Section 6.3.2 of this practice guide and in Section 4.10.3 of *Business Analysis for Practitioners: A Practice Guide.* Consistent language and syntax should be used in the models to minimize confusion and increase comprehension of requirements.

6.2.2.3 Prioritize Requirements

Requirements prioritization is an important step in managing product scope and is used to rank requirements in the order of importance. It is used to assist key stakeholders in making tradeoffs between requirements and to analyze the relative value of requirements against one another. Since it may not be feasible to implement all requirements within the project constraints, prioritization helps to focus the stakeholders on the most critical requirements based on the prioritization criteria. It is essential to define the criteria that will be used in prioritization, and this is typically accomplished during requirements management planning. Common types of criteria include:

- Value,
- Risk level,
- Complexity,
- Cost, and
- Regulatory constraints.

These criteria provide the foundation for continual prioritization as requirements evolve and change over the project life cycle. Several techniques exist that can be used to drive prioritization. Some commonly used techniques include MoSCoW, voting, and timeboxing, which are further described in Section 6.3.1.

6.2.2.4 Allocate and Derive Requirements

Requirements allocation is the process of assigning requirements to functions, solution components, and organizational entities. Requirements are subsequently allocated to specific releases or iterations. This activity occurs in the analysis process until in-scope requirements have been apportioned across the solution. Allocation helps assure that the proposed solution will be delivered in a manner and order that maximize value to the business. How requirements are allocated can change the amount of value delivered by the solution.

Deriving requirements is the process of analyzing requirements into more detail to extrapolate more granular discrete requirements and remove ambiguity. When requirements are broadly defined, they should be progressively elaborated to a greater level of detail or decomposed into multiple discrete requirements to aid in the implementation of higher-level requirements or to reduce ambiguity. This process results in derived requirements, which are important to confirm that the required functionality is present. It provides the basis for subsequent verification and validation.

6.2.2.5 Verify Requirements

Requirements should be scrutinized to confirm integrity and ensure that quality standards are being met. Requirements verification is the process of reviewing requirements to ensure the requirements are constructed properly and are error free.

Requirements verification involves conducting peer reviews and inspections to detect errors and identify inconsistencies in the requirements in order to meet quality standards.

A successful verification process requires that specific quality characteristics are known and adhered to. These characteristics serve as a set of guidelines when reviewing requirements to ensure they are of high quality. The following characteristics are present in all well-written, high-quality requirements:

- **Unambiguous.** The requirement has a single meaning and is interpreted the same way by the intended audience.
- **Consistent.** The requirement does not contradict or duplicate other requirements.
- **Correct.** The requirement accurately represents the functionality to be built as defined by the stakeholder or other requirement source.
- **Complete.** The requirement includes the necessary information and valid conditions necessary to design, build, and test the solution.
- **Measurable.** The requirement can be proven or verified through analysis, test, inspection, or demonstration.
- **Feasible.** The requirement can be implemented within the known constraints and capabilities of the operating environment.
- **Traceable.** The requirement has a unique identifier and can be referenced throughout the life cycle and requirements hierarchy.
- **Precise.** The requirement states precisely what the solution to the business problem is—no more, no less.
- **Testable.** The requirement should be written in a way that allows it to be tested.

In an adaptive life cycle where user stories typically represent requirements, the INVEST acronym can be applied to ensure the quality of the user story. INVEST encompasses the following elements:

- **Independent.** The user story should be stand-alone and avoid the creation of dependencies between user stories.
- **Negotiable.** The user story should be subject to negotiation at all times regarding its content, priority, form, and function.
- **Valuable.** The user story should only define features or functions that are valuable to the business and help solve the business problem.

- **Estimable.** The user story should be clear enough to generate a valid estimate or enable discussions that result in an estimate.
- **Small.** The user story should be small enough to be implemented within a single iteration.
- **Testable.** The user story should be independently verifiable.

6.2.2.6 Validate Requirements

Requirements are validated to ensure that the product, service, or result represents the needs of the business and relevant stakeholders. Validation is a process used to evaluate that all requirements accurately reflect the intent of the stakeholder, thereby ensuring requirements meet stakeholder expectations. Validation is typically performed by conducting a walkthrough of the requirements with stakeholders to confirm the requirements as stated are valid and will deliver the anticipated value.

6.2.3 Document and Communicate Results

Analysis is conducted with the intent of documenting the results in an accessible and consistent manner to meet the needs of the intended audience and the project life cycle being used. This documentation is developed in accordance with the requirements management plan, which defines the requirements that define the solution scope to address the business problem or opportunity. This documentation is used by the solution team so that the team understands how to build the solution. The requirements documentation may be created in various forms and levels of formality, such as specifications, written text, models, etc. These different representations should be selected based on the type of project life cycle, organizational or industry practices, and stakeholder preferences. For example, projects using adaptive (e.g., agile) or lean methodologies favor more lightweight and less extensive requirements specifications because the development environment is more collaborative and can use conversations over documentation.

6.3 Requirements Analysis Techniques

Many techniques are used to perform requirements analysis. These techniques primarily assist with prioritization and modeling of requirements.

6.3.1 Backlog Management and Prioritization

In adaptive life cycles, user stories populate a backlog and are used as a basis for prioritizing development. As user stories get closer to the top of the backlog, they should be elaborated using relevant modeling techniques to generate enough details for development to occur (known as "grooming the backlog").

Since decisions regarding priorities are often complex, a structured approach may be necessary to simplify the process. Several of these techniques are defined in Sections 6.3.1.1 through 6.3.1.3.

6.3.1.1 MoSCoW

MoSCoW, a prioritization technique, provides four possible classifications to prioritize requirements and derives its name from the first letter of each classification: must, should, could, or won't. "*must* have" means the requirement is fundamental to the success of the solution. "*should* have" defines the requirement as important, but project success does not rely on it. "*could* have" means the requirement can be eliminated without impacting the project. "*won't* have" means the requirement will not be delivered during the current release or iteration.

6.3.1.2 Voting

Voting is a participatory decision model that allows participants to distribute a predetermined number of votes to a list of requirements. The votes allocated are then used to compare the relative weight or importance of requirements to one another to establish order. There are many methods of voting available to gain active support and participation from stakeholders. Regardless of the method used, voting provides a systematic process for identifying requirements that are deemed higher-priority than others.

6.3.1.3 Timeboxing

Timeboxing ranks requirements based on the capacity of work that can be accomplished within a specified period of time. It is most often used for projects with tight schedule constraints and allows for control of the project schedule at the lowest level. If fixed cost is a concern, this technique can be modified to use money instead of time. This variation is used to determine the requirements that can be delivered within the budget constraints.

6.3.2 Modeling

The types of models used should be determined by the particular information that needs to be communicated and the audience that will receive the information. Models are used to determine what is important and valuable so that the right requirements are created. These techniques can be organized into categories, which are defined by the information that is conveyed, as described in Sections 6.3.2.1 through 6.3.2.6.

6.3.2.1 Scope Models

Scope models identify the boundaries of the project, program, product, or system under analysis. These models are used to express the features, functions, capabilities, and boundaries of the domain being analyzed. Techniques within this category are described as follows:

- **Context diagram.** A system context diagram depicts the product scope by showing the direct interactions that occur between the system, people, and other systems in a solution. It provides the inputs, outputs, and flow of information for each entity involved, which may reveal interface requirements that need to be elicited. This diagram may be represented as an architectural view within an architecture framework.

- **Ecosystem map.** An ecosystem map illustrates the components of the system, including the relationships that exist among the people, data, hardware, and software, for example. It provides a high-level depiction of the system interfaces, but not the specific requirements themselves. In contrast to the context diagram, an ecosystem map shows both direct and indirect interactions. This diagram may be represented as an operational view within an architectural framework.

- **Goal model and business objectives model.** Goal models and business objectives models are used to organize the goals, business problems, business objectives, and top-level features. These models provide a structure to specify the business requirements that trace back to the higher-level objectives. This traceability helps to quantify the value of the project based on its contribution to the business goals and objectives, which makes it easier to prioritize requirements and shape the scope of the features.

- **Feature model.** A feature model displays the organization of requirement sets (features) in logical groupings and their relationship to one another. Organizing features in this fashion supports traceability by identifying missing or redundant requirements or features.

- **Use case diagram.** A use case diagram is a graphical depiction of the in-scope use cases for a system and how an actor (stakeholder) interacts with them. Use cases do not show requirements, but help to organize requirements for analysis efforts and a requirements document. These are described in Section 6.3.2.3.

6.3.2.2 Function Models

Function models in value management/value engineering are used to organize the logic and dependency relationships between functions. These models are used to graphically represent the project, product, and process as well as identify gaps for the purpose of discovering functions that may be difficult to identify. Function models can be developed for products, projects, or processes to represent either the baseline or a future state. Function models differ from process models in that they reveal what is required to be done rather than describe how the process is or will be delivered. Function modeling techniques may include decomposition models or function/feature tree models.

- **Functional decomposition model.** A function modeling technique that identifies basic and secondary functional relationships and requirements for the current or desired future scope.

- **Function/feature tree model.** A function/feature modeling technique that identifies major functions/features and subfunction/feature relationships in a hierarchical arrangement.

These models can be used to assess cost, performance, roles, and risk dimensions, which aid in the selection and targeting of specific functions for improvement.

6.3.2.3 Process Models

Process models describe user or stakeholder interactions with a particular process or solution. Some common process models used to analyze requirements include process flows, use cases, and user stories.

- **Process flow.** A process flow outlines the activities performed, including the sequence of steps, decisions, and roles responsible for performing the step. It is typically used to display processes for the current and future states during facilitation sessions with stakeholders. This model is effective during elicitation and analysis to derive requirements, since requirements can be directly traced to individual processes.

- **Use case.** A use case describes a system's behavior from the user's perspective and provides a high-level view of the intended functionality. It helps identify functional requirements by clarifying the goals that a stakeholder needs to accomplish while interacting with a particular system. Use cases support requirements traceability and solution validation as they provide the foundation for developing test cases. A use case may be supplemented by a use case diagram that visually displays the use cases, the stakeholders who interact with the solution (actors), and the interfaces between the use cases and the actors. Use case diagrams are explained in Section 6.3.2.1.

- **User story.** A user story is a statement written in everyday language from the viewpoint of a user. It is intended to capture the new functionality or capability of a solution. A user story may contain many requirements; therefore, it can serve as a functional grouping of requirements. User stories can be used to manage, prioritize, trace, and allocate functionality to releases and iterations.

6.3.2.4 Rule Models

Rule models document business policies, business rules, and decisions that are required to be adhered to by the solution. Techniques that fall in this category include business rules catalog and decision tree/decision tables.

- **Business rules catalog.** A business rules catalog is a repository of business rules and related attributes, which define the guidelines and standards that influence the behavior of a solution. Business rules are generally documented in a type of a computation, fact, or constraint. These rules should be defined during elicitation and analysis because they could lead to functional requirements that exist to support the business rules.

- **Decision tree/decision table.** Decision trees and decision tables document a series of decisions and their associated outcomes. These models are used to represent complex business rules, including possible conditions and actions. A decision tree resembles a tree of decision points in which each branch provides a different option. It is best used to select binary choices, such as yes or no. A decision table uses a tabular format to represent decision points and outcomes and is most effective when multiple options exist. This helps stakeholders make informed decisions, which are based on expected values and outcome probabilities, and help expose gaps in the requirements to ensure that the anticipated results are achieved.

6.3.2.5 Data Models

Data models describe the specific information needs of a process or system and the transition of this information throughout its life cycle. By showing relationships between data and processes, this model provides additional details needed to extract requirements and related business rules. Techniques within this category are described as follows:

- **Entity relationship diagram.** A business model that shows the business data objects involved in a project and the relationships between those objects, including the cardinality of those relationships. Also known as a business data diagram, this model is essential for allowing business data objects to be traced directly to requirements.

- **Data flow diagram.** Data flow diagrams portray the movement of data through a system and how the data is manipulated by processes. It documents where information is stored and identifies specific inputs and outputs of processes. This documentation provides a deeper understanding of how data is used in a system leading to identifying specific data requirements.

- **Data dictionary.** A data dictionary provides a description of the fields, attributes, and properties that define the data objects relevant to the system. This structure allows information about each data element to be documented in a consistent format. Due to the large amount of detail analyzed, data dictionaries are used to capture very detailed requirements and their business rules that may have been overlooked in the elicitation process.

- **State table/state diagram.** State tables and state diagrams document the life cycle of a data object by defining the possible conditions or stages that the object may undergo within a solution. These models illustrate the transition between states, the sequence in which the transition occurs, and the events that trigger each transition.

6.3.2.6 Interface Models

Interface models document the relationships and interactions among systems and/or users within a solution. The following include some of the common interface models:

- **Report table.** A report table describes the requirements needed to develop and display information for a single report. It defines how data is manipulated and displayed to a user. This table helps specify the type of data that needs to be included in the report to ensure details are not forgotten or overlooked in the solution. It provides additional details that cannot be gleaned by reviewing a mockup.

- **System interface table.** A system interface table documents the communication flow and transfer of data between the source and target systems. This includes the specific data objects, the volume of data transferred, and the frequency of the transmission. This table is used to verify that the interface requirements accurately describe how data will be used by the system.

- **User interface flow.** A user interface flow describes communication between a user and a system. It depicts how users manipulate a system to accomplish a task. This model can be traced to other requirements models such as process flows and individual requirements of a solution.

- **Wireframe/display-action-response.** A display-action-response (DAR) model documents the manner in which a system displays data and how the system responds to actions initiated by a user. This model is typically used in conjunction with wireframes that provide screen mockups of the user interface. Wireframes and DAR models are helpful for identifying user interface requirements related to user actions and system behavior.

- **N2 diagram.** An N2 diagram is a model, represented in a tabular format, used to identify and represent the interfaces among elements of a system. This tool can be used to help identify and trace requirements that affect more than one part of a system, which generally require allocation to multiple lower-level requirements, often resulting in an iterative solution design process.

7

REQUIREMENTS MONITORING AND CONTROLLING

The requirements monitoring and controlling domain iteratively monitors the status of requirements and manages the requirements baseline over the project life cycle. In the context of the requirements process, activities include monitoring and controlling so changes to the requirements themselves are approved and managed. It should be noted that the process and related activities involved in the development and management of requirements are distinct from the project management life cycle.

The requirements traceability matrix and associated attributes created during elicitation and analysis are applied in requirements monitoring to help control the product and project scope. Traceability is updated as changes are approved. Approved requirements are baselined and tracked, to include linkages among parent and child requirements. As new requirements are identified, they are assessed for impacts to the project and product and presented to stakeholders for approval. Throughout monitoring and controlling, the status of requirements is communicated using the communication methods defined and approved within the communications management plans. This section will describe requirements monitoring and controlling success factors, activities, and techniques.

Requirements instability is a leading cause of scope creep, and the requirements monitoring and controlling activities ensure that requested changes to requirements are processed through the Perform Integrated Change Control process as described in Section 4.5 of the *PMBOK® Guide* – Fifth Edition and in greater detail in the *Practice Standard for Project Configuration Management* [6].

In an adaptive life cycle, scope is controlled during monitoring and controlling by managing the backlog. The backlog is reviewed and revised for each iteration, thereby allowing more opportunity for new requirements to be addressed. Once the scope of an iteration is decided upon, changes are managed and controlled accordingly.

Traceability provides the ability to track product requirements from their origin to the activities and deliverables that satisfy them. Traceability is "bidirectional" or "forward and backward." Not all projects require the same amount of traceability documentation, so the specific deliverables that are traceable for the project are determined during requirements management planning. Generally, the more complex projects require more traceability. A project in a heavily regulated industry or one with numerous components, interfaces, risks, and stakeholders requires more detailed traceability than a project without those characteristics.

7.1 Requirements Monitoring and Controlling Success Factors

From the start, the project management plan should include the activities required to monitor and control project baselines. The application of the overall project baseline monitoring and controlling processes to the requirements baseline should be defined in the requirements management plan, as described in Sections 4 and 7.2.

Key requirements should be identified and marked as such, and monitored continuously. These requirements, sometimes referred to as key performance indicators, are those requirements for which the inability to meet a threshold value puts the project at risk of failing to meet the business need of the organization.

7.2 Requirements Monitoring and Controlling Activities

After creating the traceability matrix during elicitation and analysis, requirements monitoring and controlling key processes include approving baseline requirements, managing changes to requirements, monitoring requirements status, and communicating results. Once the requirements baseline is established, the person primarily responsible for the requirements ensures that they are managed and that changes to the requirements are addressed through the defined change management process. Figure 7-1 describes the process flow.

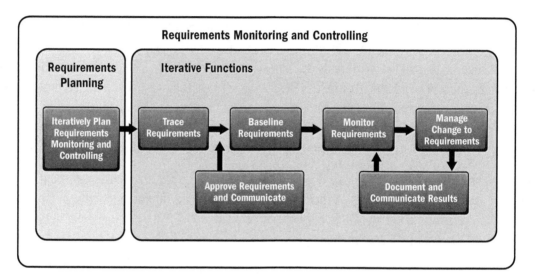

Figure 7-1. Requirements Monitoring and Controlling Activities Diagram

7.2.1 Prepare for Requirements Monitoring and Controlling

Requirements monitoring and controlling planning is completed during requirements management planning and considers interactions among the requirements elicitation, analysis, and evaluation domains. Because requirements monitoring and controlling activities occur across all of these domains, decisions about how requirements will be controlled and traced should be made before the creation of requirements and captured within the requirements management plan.

7.2.1.1 Set Up System for Managing Requirements and Traceability

Identification of the appropriate requirements management methods and tools for a project was discussed in Section 4.2.3. In order to monitor and control requirements, a tool may be purchased or used. This tool should be made available, with the appropriate training provided to the requirements management team before initiating the elicitation and analysis domains.

There is a range of tools available for creating traceability, from simple spreadsheets and tables to high-end systems that control the requirements and provide full traceability. The tools used to enable traceability should be determined at the start of the project, as traceability can quickly become complex and switching tools mid-project could present challenges.

7.2.1.2 Manage Requirements Attributes

Requirements attributes help define key information about the requirements. If using a traceability matrix, each attribute forms a column on the traceability matrix. Typical requirements attributes include, at a minimum, a unique ID, source of the requirement, version, priority, and acceptance criteria. Tools with an inherent traceability feature offer lists of common attributes. Within the Requirements Monitoring and Controlling process, requirements attributes are maintained along with requirements. Some attribute changes may initiate the change control process, such as a requirement that was originally deemed out of scope becoming in-scope or a requirement moving from a low level of priority to a high priority. The change control process should outline which requirements attributes will require initiation of the change control process if changed after requirements are baselined.

7.2.1.3 Maintain Traceability

The necessary level of traceability should be determined during planning and tailored to meet project needs.

7.2.2 Create Traceability Matrix

The process of creating the requirements traceability matrix is performed in parallel with the elicitation and analysis of requirements. When a requirement is written, the associated attributes and linkages should also be captured in the traceability matrix. To create such traceability after a requirement is created or updated could be difficult and important linkages and information could be lost. The basic elements of a traceability matrix are defined in more detail in Section 7.3.3.

7.2.3 Approve and Baseline Requirements

Once the requirements and associated traceability attributes have been collected and documented, it is critical that they are approved. Organizations and projects vary in how requirements are approved. Stakeholder approval to the level of formality required establishes a requirements baseline. In an adaptive approach, baselining is an iterative process focused on release and iteration planning. This baseline is traced and monitored throughout the process.

The requirements baseline is the boundary that contains the approved product requirements for the project, project phase, iteration, increment, release, or any other part of a project. The baseline provides a mechanism for comparison, thereby allowing the project team to recognize that a change has occurred. In an adaptive life cycle, baselining requirements is performed by maintaining the product backlog.

Once the requirements have been baselined, any suggested change to requirements initiates the change management process. Changes need to be analyzed, which typically involves performing an impact analysis to evaluate the proposed change in relation to how it will affect other requirements, the product, the project, and the program. Additional information on impact analysis can be found in Section 7.3.2.

There can be less formality in approving requirements in an adaptive approach, yet there should still be some norm or informal agreement on what should be approved, how it should be approved, and when it should be approved. The product owner is the primary point of contact for adaptive projects and is, therefore, ultimately responsible for approving requirements.

7.2.4 Manage Requirements Change Requests

A change request process should be defined in the planning domain. Managing change requests involves following the defined process for the project to ensure that changes are managed and requirements are updated only once the approved change management protocols are followed.

In an adaptive life cycle, the defined change request process commonly adds new requirements to the backlog, and then adds planning sessions for follow-up iterations or sprints to review the entire backlog and use a prioritization process to determine the next set of features for the subsequent iteration or sprint. This approach provides multiple opportunities to address new or modified requirements over the course of a project.

The *Practice Standard for Project Configuration Management* defines in detail the configuration change management process. Applying configuration change management principles may provide a number of assurances, including:

- The correct version of the configuration item is in use by the project team;
- Changes to configuration items are made only by authorized individuals;
- A planned means of notifying stakeholders of approved changes to configuration items is in place; and
- A record of configuration item changes is kept to support auditing and project closure activities.

PMI defines the following individual phases of the configuration change management process in the *Practice Standard for Project Configuration Management*:

- Establish baseline,
- Submit change request,
- Verify change request,
- Evaluate impacts,
- Review decision and plan,
- Implement change if approved, and
- Conclude change process.

Impacts of this process should be communicated and monitored (see also Section 7.2.6).

7.2.5 Monitor Requirements Status

The current state of requirements should be monitored in the requirements monitoring and controlling domain.

7.2.6 Document and Communicate Results

Communicating the project and product requirements baseline and effort keeps project stakeholders apprised of the current state and maintains a good level of collaboration. This is especially important with the increasing complexity of projects and programs. The overall state of the requirements management work, key requirements metrics, and overall status of requirements fulfillment should be captured and communicated to stakeholders in accordance with the project communications management plan. The metrics to be captured and communicated in requirements monitoring and controlling may be defined in the planning domain. If the metric to be monitored changes, then updates to the requirements management plan should be made. Measurements are taken over the course of the project to address the metrics, and results are shared with stakeholders on an ongoing basis.

The following are the updates captured during the requirements monitoring and controlling domain:

- **Update requirements baseline.** All requirements updates should be captured and placed under configuration control as indicated in the requirements management plan. In addition, requirements traceability updates should be captured and the configuration should be managed in accordance with the requirements management plan.

- **Capture change requests.** Change requests for all requirements should be captured and placed under configuration control as indicated in the requirements management plan. In addition to the change requests, the impact analysis and any other documents created during the change request process should be captured. The status and disposition of change requests should be readily available and monitored through change logs.

7.3 Requirements Monitoring and Controlling Techniques

Some of the techniques used to perform requirements monitoring and controlling are listed in this section. These techniques primarily assist with assessing and visualizing impacts to requirements changes.

7.3.1 Dependency Analysis

Requirements are often related to other requirements; therefore, sometimes a requirement cannot be satisfied in a solution without the other requirements being present. Dependency analysis is a technique that is used to discover dependent relationships. Once analyzed, the set of requirements are recorded in the traceability matrix by grouping dependent requirements together. Some requirements management tools illustrate the dependencies visually by creating traceability trees.

7.3.2 Impact Analysis

When a requirement change is proposed, it is necessary to complete an impact analysis to evaluate the proposed change in relation to how it will affect other requirements, the product, the project, and the program. The impact analysis assesses a proposed change that includes the identification of the risks associated with the change, the work required to incorporate the change, and the schedule and cost implications. One should consider how a proposed change may impact the value of the solution to be delivered and whether the change continues to address the business need and objectives that were approved by the stakeholders. A key benefit of completing an impact analysis is that it allows for changes within the project to be considered in an integrated fashion, thereby reducing project and product risk, which often arises from changes being made without consideration to the effect on the program, project, and the end product.

7.3.3 Traceability Matrix

Organizations often trace their requirements using a structure called a traceability matrix. A traceability matrix is a grid that links product requirements from their origin to the deliverables that satisfy them. The implementation of a requirements traceability matrix supports the goal that each requirement adds business value by linking it to the business and project objectives. It provides a means to track requirements throughout the project life cycle, helping to ensure that approved requirements are delivered at the end of the project. The matrix also provides a structure for managing changes, thereby helping to manage the product scope.

7.3.4 Change Control Boards

A change control board (CCB) is a formally chartered group of stakeholders responsible for reviewing, evaluating, approving, delaying, or rejecting changes to the project in addition to recording and communicating such decisions. Not all projects require the use of a CCB. A project in a heavily regulated industry or one with numerous components, interfaces, risks, and stakeholders may require the use of a formal CCB more than a project without those characteristics.

The CCB is often the ultimate source for approving requirements when there is a significant scope change beyond the project sponsor's ability to approve. Once approved requirements are baselined, any changes are proposed through the CCB. The CCB may choose to have change requests under a prescribed dollar amount approved by business stakeholders and/or the sponsor, and change requests over the threshold approved by the CCB. Those thresholds usually are defined by impact on cost, schedule, or deliverables and should be defined in the requirements management plan.

SOLUTION EVALUATION

Solution evaluation is the domain of business analysis concerned with the activities performed to validate a solution that is about to be or that has already been implemented. Evaluation determines how well a solution meets the business needs expressed by stakeholders, including delivering value to the customer. Evaluation of an implemented solution can also identify new or changed requirements that may lead to solution refinement or new solutions.

Evaluation activities generally support verification and validation of the solution. A well-defined set of requirements should reflect an agreement with the stakeholder(s) on a set of measurable outcomes that are most likely to meet the stakeholder needs. Testing, analysis, and other means of demonstrating that the agreed-upon requirements have been met (verification activities) work alongside activities that demonstrate the suitability of the solution for its intended purpose (validation activities). Stated more simply, validation answers the question, "Did we do the right thing?," while verification addresses, "Did we do it correctly?"

Different organizations and communities of practice may use different terminology or may assign these functions to different parts of the project team. However, the concepts and associated methods for ensuring that the delivered product meets stakeholder needs are common to many projects. Organizations may choose to have an independent third party that is not involved in the development of the product conduct verification and validation, otherwise known as independent verification and validation (IV&V).

8.1 Solution Evaluation Success Factors

The success factors for evaluation involve clearly defining and understanding how the evaluation processes will be iteratively performed, and how these processes affect each other.

8.1.1 Approach Evaluation as a Process

Evaluation is most successful when treated as a process rather than a discrete event. Evaluation forms a basis for stakeholder acceptance as solutions or segments of a solution are implemented. Acceptance criteria, when established early, can serve as a foundation for evaluating candidate solutions, are useful in the development of verification strategies, and can identify which areas of a solution will need the most testing.

8.2 Solution Evaluation Activities

The key processes involved in evaluation include planning, documenting, and communicating results.

8.2.1 Plan for Evaluation

Planning for evaluation should begin in requirements management planning early in the project and should consider the interactions with other project management related activities.

Evaluation planning includes the selection of specific techniques used to evaluate that the solution delivered is performing as intended and ensuring the business needs and value are still being addressed. A common, good practice is to include selected evaluation techniques as part of the requirements management plan. Evaluation activities should also be reflected in the overall project baseline.

8.2.2 Validation During Solution Evaluation

The validation process conducted during solution evaluation ensures the solution is working as intended and meets the stakeholder and business needs on which its documented requirements are based. Some approaches to validation attempt to draw a distinction between validation of the requirements set (accomplished during analysis) and validation of the solution or component of the solution.

For a predictive project life cycle, validate the solution at the end of the project life cycle either immediately before release or at an agreed-upon time after release. For an iterative or adaptive project life cycle, validation is performed at the end of every iteration, sprint, or release, when the team provides production-ready functionality for the stakeholders to evaluate. For many projects, validation is a prerequisite to solution acceptance.

This step serves as a final check on demonstrating that the product does, in fact, meet its intended business need in the user, stakeholder, or organizational context.

8.2.3 Document and Communicate Results

There are many available methods to document and communicate the evaluation results. The approach should be selected early in a project and documented in the requirements management plan. The documentation approach may depend on factors such as the size and complexity of the project, the nature of the solution (e.g., software, hardware, or service), contractual or regulatory constraints, stakeholder preferences, or the predictive or adaptive nature of the project life cycle.

For most projects, a combination of communication approaches is used to convey not only the raw evaluation results, but also to inform solution decisions.

8.3 Solution Evaluation Techniques

A wide variety of evaluation techniques exist and are selected and applied differently depending on the community of knowledge, industry, or sector. Many commonly used techniques can be grouped into broad categories based on the type of information evaluated. Many of the techniques described in this section are also applicable to the requirements elicitation and analysis domains. When applied to elicitation and/or analysis, the tools are generally being used to identify and document a set of requirements that, if met, will meet the needs identified during the needs assessment domain. When applied to evaluation, the same tools may be used to validate the full solution or a segment of a solution and how well the solution meets the underlying business need and value to the customer. For additional information on when and how to validate solution results, refer to Section 6.6 of *Business Analysis for Practitioners: A Practice Guide.*

8.3.1 Solicit Inputs

One general approach to evaluating a solution is to solicit input from stakeholders, end users, or people with specific related expertise to validate that the product, service, or result is performing as intended. A variety of formal and informal techniques exists, including reviews, focus groups, surveys, brainstorming, checklists, multivoting, or the Delphi technique. Usage context documentation generated during the requirements elicitation and/or analysis domains may also be useful tools to support the collection of subjective inputs.

Another common class of techniques used for evaluation is examination. This is a broad group of techniques that includes testing and demonstration.

- **Testing.** Testing, either exploratory or user acceptance testing, validates that the solution meets the defined acceptance criteria.
- **Demonstration.** This examines the solution, generally by operating it, to prove or show that it meets its intended functions.

8

PROJECT OR PHASE CLOSURE

The outcomes of solution evaluation activities lead to a go/no-go decision, and if a go decision is reached, signoff of the solution is obtained. Signoff can be either formal or informal.

Evaluating the long-term performance of the solution is part of assessing the business benefits realized by implementing the solution, which is described in Section 6.10 of *Business Analysis for Practitioners: A Practice Guide,* and occurs after the project or phase is closed.

Project or phase closure is the process of finalizing all activities across all of the Project Management Process Groups to formally complete the project or phase. This work is the responsibility of the project or program manager and addressees the transition of the product, service, or result from the project life cycle. Closure may include:

- Documenting lessons learned and providing knowledge transfer,
- Supporting transition to operations, and
- Enabling the organization to sustain long-term performance benefits over time.

Organizational process asset updates are completed for the project, as they are considered to be an output of the process. Project or phase closure includes all planned activities necessary for administrative closure of the program, project, or iteration, including:

- Activities necessary to satisfy completion or exit criteria for the program, project, or iteration, including the evaluation of the acceptance criteria performed during the solution evaluation domain;
- Activities necessary to transfer the product, service, or result to the next program, project, or iteration or to production and/or operations; and
- Activities necessary to collect project or iteration records, audit project success or failure, gather lessons learned, and archive related information for future use by the organization.

If the program, project, or iteration was terminated prior to completion, the formal documentation indicates why the initiative was terminated and formalizes the procedures for transferring project artifacts to another project or program, or archiving those artifacts for possible reuse.

9.1 Project or Phase Closure Success Factors

The success factors discussed in Sections 9.1.1 through 9.1.3 are considered vital to maximize the effectiveness of this process.

9.1.1 Documented Transition Plan

The transition plan provides the transition team with the project files, closure documents, and historical information for the project as a part of the transition for project or phase closure.

9.1.2 Final Customer Acceptance

Customer acceptance, internal or external, allows the project to transition into closure activities and allows the organization to transition to long-term performance benefits realization monitoring.

9.1.3 Defined Metrics to Measure Benefits Realization

Metrics measuring the benefits realized by the product, service, or result provide valuable feedback to the stakeholders. This feedback loop may enable improvements to the solution and increase the maturity of the organization, thereby leading to increases in project success.

9.2 Project or Phase Closure Activities

Closure comprises four primary activities, as described in Sections 9.2.1 through 9.2.4.

9.2.1 Document

Most organizations find it important to document whether they are satisfied with the product, service, or result at the end of a program, project, or iteration. The documentation may be updated once long-term performance benefits have been realized, but this is the responsibility of business analysis and considered to be a post-project activity as discussed in Section 6 of *Business Analysis for Practitioners: A Practice Guide*.

9.2.2 Reuse

Reuse involves leveraging existing knowledge across projects and programs with similar needs. Requirements reuse should be planned for during business analysis planning and performed throughout the various phases of the project. When reuse is planned and executed effectively during the project or program, it takes advantage of work done previously, which may result in improved productivity, lower costs, increased service delivery, and reduced rework.

9.2.3 Lessons Learned and Providing for Knowledge Transfer

Collecting and documenting lessons learned is a critical means of transferring knowledge to other programs, projects, or iterations. Lessons learned are generally planned during planning domains and collected at the end of a program, project, or iteration or after a critical activity or milestone. For adaptive life cycles, lessons learned are often captured during retrospectives, which are often scheduled on a regular basis or conducted when a body of work is completed, such as the conclusion of an iteration or at the end of a project phase.

To apply these lessons learned, it is essential that the information be easily accessible and institutionalized into the governing organization and its processes and procedures.

According to PMI's *Pulse of the Profession*® research findings, organizations that are most effective at knowledge transfer improve project outcomes by nearly 35% [7]. These organizations are also three times as likely to have a formal knowledge transfer process: 92% compared to 33%. Organizations that are good at knowledge transfer conduct the following steps of the knowledge transfer life cycle:

- **Identifying.** Determining what knowledge needs to be transferred.
- **Capturing.** Accumulating the essential knowledge that needs to be transferred.
- **Sharing.** Establishing methods for transferring the knowledge.
- **Applying.** Using the knowledge that is transferred.
- **Assessing.** Evaluating the benefits of the knowledge that is transferred.

Capturing lessons learned and providing for enabling knowledge transfer provides the means to continuously improve the project life cycle process, activities, and techniques.

9.2.4 Support Transition to Operations

Programs, projects, or iterations deliver benefits by enhancing current capabilities or developing new capabilities that support the sponsoring organization's strategic goals and objectives. Benefits may be realized incrementally upon completion of a project or iteration or may be realized over the longer term. Transition of the product, service, or result to operations, whether done incrementally or at the end of the program or project, is an important step in preparing the solution to realize the expected benefits of the program or project.

Transition to operations may be a formal activity between functions within a single organization or may involve an agreement with an entity outside the organization. The receiving entity should have a clear understanding of the capabilities or results to be transitioned and what is required for the entity to successfully sustain or attain benefits.

9.3 Project or Phase Closure Techniques

Various techniques can be used to finalize the project or phase closure activities. These techniques may be used separately or together. The most commonly used techniques are described in Sections 9.3.1 through 9.3.3.

9.3.1 Expert Judgment

Expert judgment is applied when performing administrative closure activities. These experts ensure the closure of the program, project, or iteration is performed to the appropriate standards. Expertise is available from many sources, including but not limited to:

- Business analysis and requirements professionals,
- Project management office, and
- Professional and technical associations.

9.3.2 Analytical Techniques

Many of the analytical techniques previously described may also be used to determine the limitations of the implemented solution.

Other examples of analytical techniques used in project or phase closure may include:

- Benchmarking,
- Gap analysis,
- Regression analysis, and
- Trend analysis.

9.3.3 Meetings

Meetings are used to discuss and address topics related to project or phase closure activities. These meetings may be face-to-face, virtual, formal, or informal, and normally involve knowledge transfer and documentation of lessons learned. In adaptive life cycles, lessons learned meetings are generally referred to as retrospectives and are conducted at the end of each iteration. These meetings are used to understand the successes and challenges of an initiative, as well as to identify areas of improvement.

APPENDIX X1
CONTRIBUTORS AND REVIEWERS OF REQUIREMENTS MANAGEMENT: A PRACTICE GUIDE

The Project Management Institute is grateful to all of these individuals for their support and acknowledges their contributions to the project management profession.

X1.1 Core Committee

The following individuals served as members, were contributors of text or concepts, or served as leaders within the Project Core Committee:

James F. Carilli, PfMP, PgMP, PMP (Vice Chair)
Shika Carter, PgMP, PMP, CBAP
Wanda Curlee, PfMP, PgMP, PMP
Brian L. Grafsgaard, PfMP, PgMP, PMP (Chair)
Joanne Muszynski, PMP, CSM
Rebecca Onuschak, PMP, CSEP
Craig L. Squires, CVS
Dennis K. Van Gemert, PMP, CSEP, AFAIAA
Kristin L. Vitello, Standards Project Specialist

PMI would also like to thank the following organization for its contribution: Stellar Solutions, Inc.

X1.2 Content Reviewers

In addition to the members of the Committee, the following individuals provided their review and recommendations on the draft of this practice guide:

Ashutosh Agarwal, PgMP, PMP
Shyamprakash K. Agrawal, PgMP, PMP
Vahid Azadmanesh, MBA, PMP
M. Salman Bilal, PfMP, PMI-PBA
Steve Blais, PMP, PMI-PBA
Greta Blash, PMP, PMI-PBA
Marc Burlereaux, PgMP, PMP

Sergio Luis Conte, PhD
Michael J. Frenette, PMP, CMC
Lars Grossmann, PhD, PMP
Candase Hokanson
Prasad Kamath, PfMP, CBAP
Gerhard Kloimwieder, PMP
Ronald Kohl
Ginger Levin, PhD, PgMP, PMP
Peter Lefterov, CBAP
Vanina Mangano, PMP, PMI-RMP
Mohammed Mansoor, PfMP, PgMP
Eric E. Nichols
Beth Ouellette, PgMP, PBA
Jose L. Fernandez Sanchez, PhD
Jenny Saunders BSc hons, ICP-BVA
Guy Schleffer, PfMP, PgMP
Carolina Gabriela Spindola, PMP, SSBB
Beth Stana, PMP
Angela M. Wick, PMP, PBA
David Wilf

X1.3 PMI Standards Program Member Advisory Group (MAG)

The following individuals served as members of the PMI Standards Program Member Advisory Group during development of *Requirements Management: A Practice Guide:*

Cyndi Snyder Dionisio, MBA, PMP
Larry Goldsmith MBA, PMP
Hagit Landman, PMP, PMI-SP
Yvan Petit, PhD, PfMP
Chris Stevens, PhD
Dave Violette, MPM, PMP
John Zlockie, MBA, PMP, PMI Standards Manager

X1.4 Production Staff

Special mention is due to the following employees of PMI:

Donn Greenberg, Manager, Publications
Roberta Storer, Product Editor
Barbara Walsh, Publications Production Supervisor

APPENDIX X2
SUGGESTED ADDITIONAL READING MATERIALS

The following are suggested additional reading materials:

Alexander, I. F., and Beus-Dukic, L. 2009. *Discovering Requirements: How to Specify Products and* Services. New York: Wiley.

Beatty, J., and Chen, A. 2012. *Visual Models for Software Requirements (Developer Best Practices)*. Redmond, WA: Microsoft Press.

Beatty, J., and Wiegers, K. 2013. *Software Requirements*, 3rd ed. Redmond, WA: Microsoft Press.

Cohn, M. 2006. *Agile Estimating and Planning.* Upper Saddle River, NJ: Pearson Education.

Cohn, M. 2009. *Succeeding with Agile: Software Development Using Scrum.* Essex, UK: Addison-Wesley Professional.

Crispin, L., and Gregory, J. 1009. *Agile Testing: A Practical Guide for Testers and Agile Teams.* Upper Saddle River, NJ: Pearson Education.

Davis, A. M. 2005. *Just Enough Requirements Management: Where Software Development Meets Marketing.* New York: Dorset House Publishing.

Gottesdiener, E. 2002. *Requirements by Collaboration: Workshops for Defining Needs.* Boston: Addison-Wesley Professional.

Gottesdiener, E. 2005. *The Software Requirements Memory Jogger: A Pocket Guide to Help Software and Business Teams Develop and Manage Requirements.* Salem, NH: Goal/QPC Inc.

Gottesdiener, E., and Gorman, M. 2012. *Discover to Deliver: Agile Product Planning and Analysis.* Sudbury, MA: EBG Consulting, Inc.

Hass, K. B., Wessels, D., and Brennan, K. 2007. *Getting It Right: Business Requirement Analysis Tools and Techniques.* Vienna, VA: Management Concepts.

Kulak, D., and Guiney, E. 2000. *Use Cases: Requirements in Context.* New York: ACM Press.

Larson, E., and Larson, R. *Practitioner's Guide to Requirements Management* (2nd ed.). Minneapolis, MN: Watermark Learning.

Leffingwell, D., and Widrig, D. W. 2003. *Managing Software Requirements: A Use Case Approach* (2nd ed.). Boston, MA: Addison-Wesley Professional.

Lieberman, B. A. 2006. *The Art of Software Modeling.* Boca Raton, FL: Auerbach Publications.

Miller, R. E. 2009. *The Quest for Software Requirements.* Milwaukee, WI: Maven Mark Books.

Project Management Institute. 2015. *PMI Lexicon of Project Management Terms* (ver 3). Newtown Square, PA: Author.

Robertson, S., and Robertson, J. C. 2004. *Requirements-Led Project Management: Discovering David's Slingshot.* Essex, UK: Addison-Wesley Professional.

Robertson, S., and Robertson, J. 2005. *Mastering the Requirements Process: Getting Requirements Right* (3rd ed.). Boston, MA: Addison-Wesley Professional.

Rumbaugh, J., Jacobson, I., and Booch, G. 2004. *The Unified Modeling Language Reference Manual* (2nd ed.). Essex, UK: Addison-Wesley Professional.

Schneider, G., and Winters, J. 2001. *Applying Use Cases, A Practical Guide*. Upper Saddle River, NJ: Pearson Education.

Thayer, R. H., and Dorfman, M. 1990. *System and Software Requirements Engineering*. Washington, DC: IEEE Computer Society Press.

Wake, B. 2003. *INVEST in Good Stories, and SMART Tasks*. Retrieved from http://xp123.com/articles/invest-in-good-stories-and-smart-tasks/

Weinberg, G. M., and Gauss, D. C. 1989. *Exploring Requirements: Quality Before Design*. New York: Dorset House.

Wiegers, K. 2005. *More About Software Requirements: Thorny Issues and Practical Advice (Developer Best Practices)*. Redmond, WA: Microsoft Press.

Young, R. R. 2001. *Effective Requirements Practices*. Essex, UK: Addison-Wesley Professional.

APPENDIX X3
REQUIREMENTS MANAGEMENT ASSOCIATED
COMMUNITIES OF PRACTICE

Requirements Management: A Practice Guide identifies the commonalities between four requirements development and management communities of practice. The communities of practice that were researched and consulted during the development of this guide include business analysis, systems engineering, software engineering, and value engineering. PMI research confirmed significant overlap between these communities of practice. The following are brief descriptions of each community of practice that was researched during the development of this practice guide.

X3.1 Software Engineering

Software engineering is the application of engineering to the design, development, and maintenance of computer software. Software engineering is divided into 10 related disciplines. The first of these subdisciplines is requirements engineering. This includes the elicitation, analysis, specification, and validation of requirements for software. This practice guide presents each of these subdisciplines along with the needs assessment, requirements management planning, and requirements monitoring and controlling domains.

For more information see: *Software Extension to the PMBOK® Guide Fifth Edition.* [8].

X3.2 Systems Engineering

Systems engineering is a community of knowledge that emphasizes the satisfaction of business and technical needs through the delivery of a product, service, or result in the form of a system. The focus on solutions in the form of systems results in a structured, holistic approach to defining and managing the elements of the system and its interfaces (interface requirements) and interdependencies. Concept of operations (CONOPS) uses the solution life cycle as a framework to integrate the needs of the stakeholders and users that will interact with the solution while ensuring breadth of elicitation. Requirements development and management over the system life cycle is a significant part of the overall systems engineering approach.

For additional information, see:

- *Systems Engineering Handbook: A Guide for System Life Cycle Processes and Activities*, version 3.2.2 [9], and
- *15288:2008 – IEEE/ISO/IEC Systems and Software Engineering – System Life Cycle Processes* [10].

X3.3 Value Management/Value Engineering

Value management/value engineering, as defined by the *PMBOK® Guide* – Fifth Edition, is a technique used to optimize project life cycle costs, save time, increase profits, improve quality, expand market share, solve problems, and/or use resources more effectively. This technique is applied by multidisciplinary teams to a planned or conceptual scope for a product, project, or process. Its purpose is to analyze and understand an established baseline of existing or proposed functions and requirements to develop additional ideas and alternatives to optimize the use of resources, build team consensus through the participation in the work phases, and identify gaps and opportunities for improvement. Therefore, this technique is most useful when applied in the early phase of the project when the general scope of requirements is understood well enough to develop alternatives to the baseline, and can be used at the project, program, or portfolio level. To use this technique, follow a formal and systematic process following a job plan that includes function analysis with a multidisciplinary team and led by an expert experienced in the methodology.

For additional information, see:

- *Value Methodology Standard* [11],
- *Value Methodology Body of Knowledge* [12],
- *A Framework for Value Management Practice* [13], and
- *ASTM E1699-14: Standard Practice for Performing Value Engineering (VE)/Value Analysis (VA) of Projects, Products and Processes* [14].

REFERENCES

[1] Project Management Institute. 2013. *A Guide to the Project Management Body of Knowledge (PMBOK® Guide) –* Fifth Edition. Newtown Square, PA: Author.

[2] Project Management Institute. 2015. *Business Analysis for Practitioners: A Practice Guide.* Newtown Square, PA: Author.

[3] Project Management Institute. 2014. *Pulse of the Profession® In-Depth Report on Requirements Management: A Core Competency for Project and Program Success.* Available from http://www.pmi.org /learning/pulse.aspx

[4] Project Management Institute. 2013. *The Standard for Program Management –* Third Edition. Newtown Square, PA: Author.

[5] Project Management Institute. 2013. *The Standard for Portfolio Management –* Third Edition. Newtown Square, PA: Author.

[6] Project Management Institute. 2007. *Practice Standard for Project Configuration Management.* Newtown Square, PA: Author.

[7] Project Management Institute. 2015. Pulse of the Profession®: Capturing the Value of Project Management Through Knowledge Transfer. Available from http://www.pmi.org/learning/pulse.aspx

[8] Project Management Institute. 2014. *Software Extension to the PMBOK® Guide Fifth Edition.* Newtown Square, PA: Author.

[9] INCOSE. 2012. *Systems Engineering Handbook: A Guide for System Life Cycle Processes and Activities*, ver 3.2.2. San Diego, CA: Author.

[10] IEEE. 2008. *IEEE/ISO/IEC 15288:2008: Systems and Software Engineering—System Life Cycle Processes.* Piscataway, NJ: Author

[11] SAVE International. 2015. *Value Methodology Standard.* Dayton, OH: Author.

[12] SAVE International. 2008. *Value Methodology Body of Knowledge.* Dayton, OH: Author.

[13] Thiry, M. 2013. *A Framework for Value Management Practice*, 2nd ed. Newtown Square, PA: Project Management Institute.

[14] ASTM. 2014. *ASTM E1699-14: Standard Practice for Performing Value Engineering (VE)/Value Analysis (VA) of Projects, Products and Processes.* West Conshohocken, PA: Author.

GLOSSARY

Acceptance Criteria. A set of conditions that is required to be met before deliverables are accepted. [Note: In requirements management, acceptance criteria are built to evaluate the product requirements and solution.]

Activity. A distinct, scheduled portion of work performed during the course of a project.

Adaptive Life Cycle. A project life cycle, also known as a change-driven or agile method, that is intended to facilitate change and requires a high degree of ongoing stakeholder involvement.

Affinity Diagram. A group creativity technique that allows large numbers of ideas to be classified into groups for review and analysis.

Architecture. A method to describe an organization by mapping its essential characteristics, such as people, locations, processes, applications, data, and technology.

Assumption. A factor that is considered to be true, real, or certain, without proof or demonstration.

Backlog. A listing of product requirements and deliverables to be completed, written as stories, and prioritized by the business to manage and organize the project's work.

Baseline. The approved version of a work product that can be changed only through formal change control procedures and is used as a basis for comparison.

Benchmarking. The comparison of actual or planned practices, such as processes and operations, to those of comparable organizations to identify best practices, generate ideas for improvement, and provide a basis for measuring performance.

Brainstorming. A general data-gathering and creativity technique that is used to identify risks, ideas, or solutions to issues by using a group of team members or subject matter experts.

Business Analysis. The set of activities performed to identify business needs; recommend relevant solutions; and elicit, document, and manage requirements.

Business Analysis Approach. A description of how the business analysis process will be conducted for the project or program. The business analysis approach is documented in the business analysis plan.

Business Analysis Plan. A subplan of the project management plan that defines the business analysis approach, including the tasks that will be performed, the deliverables that will be produced, the roles required to carry out the process, and process decisions regarding how requirement-related decisions will be made; how requirement priorities will be set; how changes to requirements will be proposed, approved, and managed; how requirements will be validated, verified, monitored, and traced; and how business analysis communication will be performed.

Business Analysis Planning. The domain of business analysis that involves planning all of the business analysis activities and reaching the necessary process decisions required for running an effective business analysis process for a program or project.

Business Case. A documented economic feasibility study used to establish the validity of the benefits of a selected component lacking sufficient definition and used as a basis for the authorization of further project management activities.

Business Need. The impetus for a change in an organization, based on an existing problem or opportunity. The business need provides the rationale for initiating a project or program.

Business Objectives Model. A business analysis model that relates the business problems, business objectives, and top-level features. This model encompasses the justification for a project.

Business Requirements. Requirements that describe the higher-level needs of the organization, such as the business issues or opportunities, and which provide the rationale for why a project is being undertaken.

Business Rules. Constraints about how the organization wants to operate. These constraints are usually enforced by data and/or processes and are under the jurisdiction of the business.

Business Rules Catalog. A business analysis model that details all of the business rules and their related attributes.

Business Value. A concept that is unique to each organization and includes tangible and intangible elements. In requirements management, business value is considered the return, in the form of time, money, goods, or intangibles in return for something exchanged.

Capability. The ability to add value or achieve objectives in an organization through a function, process, service, or other proficiency.

Cause-and-Effect Diagram. A decomposition technique that helps trace an undesirable effect back to its root cause. See also *fishbone diagram.*

Change Control. A process whereby modifications to documents, deliverables, or baselines associated with the project are identified, documented, approved, or rejected.

Change Control Board (CCB). A formally chartered group responsible for reviewing, evaluating, approving, delaying, or rejecting changes to the project and for recording and communicating such decisions.

Change Request. A formal proposal to modify any document, deliverable, or baseline.

Charter. See *project charter.*

Communications Management Plan. A component of the project, program, or portfolio management plan that describes how, when, and by whom information about the project will be administered and disseminated.

Concept of Operations (CONOPS). A document that is used to describe the characteristics and capabilities of a proposed system and to communicate the system need to all stakeholders in enough detail to ensure the proposed architecture meets its intent and stakeholder buy-in is achieved.

Configuration Management. A collection of formal documented processes, templates, and documentation used to apply governance to changes to the product, service, result, or subcomponent being developed.

Constraint. A limiting factor that affects the execution of a project, program, portfolio, or process.

Context Diagram. A visual depiction of the product scope showing a business system (process, equipment, computer system, etc.) and how people and other systems (actors) interact with it.

Data Dictionary. A business analysis model that catalogs the attributes of specific data objects.

Data Flow Diagram. A business analysis model that combines processes, systems, and data to show how data flows through a solution.

Decision Table. An analysis model that uses a tabular format to display complex business rules by representing decision points in the upper rows and outcomes in the bottom rows with the purpose of providing all combinations of choices.

Decision Tree. An analysis model that shows business rules associated with complex branching logic. Rules are depicted by modeling the decisions and their outcomes in a tree structure.

Decomposition Diagram. See *decomposition model.*

Decomposition Model. A model that is used to divide and subdivide a high-level concept into lower-level concepts, for example, dividing the project scope and project deliverables into smaller, more manageable parts for the purpose of analysis. Also known as decomposition diagram.

Deliverable. Any unique and verifiable product, result, or capability to perform a service that is required to be produced to complete a process, phase, or project.

Delphi Technique. An information-gathering technique used as a way to reach a consensus of experts on a subject. Experts on the subject participate in this technique anonymously. A facilitator uses a questionnaire to solicit ideas about the important project points related to the subject. The responses are summarized and are then recirculated to the experts for further comment. Consensus may be reached in a few rounds of this process. The Delphi technique helps reduce bias in the data and keeps any one person from having undue influence on the outcome.

Dependency Analysis. A technique that is used to discover dependent relationships.

Document Analysis. An elicitation technique that analyzes existing documentation and identifies information relevant to the requirements.

Ecosystem Map. A business analysis model that shows the systems involved in a project and how they interrelate with each other.

Elicitation. See *requirements elicitation.*

Entity Relationship Diagram. A business analysis model that shows the business data objects involved in a project and the relationships between those objects, including the cardinality of those relationships.

Estimate. A quantitative assessment of the likely amount or outcome. It is usually applied to project costs, resources, effort, and durations and is usually preceded by a modifier (i.e., preliminary, conceptual, feasibility, order-of-magnitude, definitive). It should always include some indication of accuracy (e.g., $\pm x\%$).

Evaluation. See *solution evaluation.*

Expert Judgment. Judgment provided based upon expertise in an application area, Knowledge Area, discipline, industry, etc., as appropriate for the activity being performed. Such expertise may be provided by any group or person with specialized education, knowledge, skill, experience, or training.

Facilitated Workshops. An elicitation technique using focused sessions that bring key cross-functional stakeholders together to define product requirements. In requirements management, facilitated workshops use a structured meeting that is led by a skilled, neutral facilitator, in which a carefully selected group of stakeholders collaborate to explore and evaluate product requirements.

Feature. A set of related requirements typically described as a short phrase.

Feature Model. A business analysis model that shows the first, second, and third level of features involved in a project.

Fishbone Diagram. A version of a cause-and-effect diagram that depicts a problem and its root causes in a visual manner. It uses a fish image, listing the problem at the head, with causes and subcauses of the problem represented as bones of the fish. See also *cause-and-effect diagram.*

Focus Groups. An elicitation technique that brings together prequalified stakeholders and subject matter experts to learn about their expectations and attitudes about a proposed product, service, or result.

Functional Requirements. Requirements that describe the behaviors of a product.

Gap Analysis. A technique for understanding the gap between current capabilities and needed capabilities. Filling the gap is what comprises a solution recommendation.

Grooming the Backlog. A process used on agile projects where the product team works with the product owner to gain more depth about the user stories in the backlog list. A groomed backlog is an input for sprint planning meetings, which are used to determine which user stories to cover in the next iteration.

Impact Analysis. A technique for evaluating a change in relation to how it will affect other requirements, the product, the program, and the project.

Interviews. A formal or informal approach to elicit information from a group of stakeholders by asking questions and documenting the responses provided by the interviewees.

Issue. A point or matter in question or in dispute, or a point or matter that is not settled and is under discussion or over which there are opposing views or disagreements. See also *opportunity, threat,* and *risk.*

Iterative Life Cycle. A project life cycle where the project scope is generally determined early in the project life cycle, but time and cost estimates are routinely modified as the project team's understanding of the product increases. Iterations develop the product through a series of repeated cycles, while increments successively add to the functionality of the product.

Kanban. An adaptive life cycle in which project work items are pulled from a backlog and started when other project work items are completed. Kanban also establishes work-in-progress limits to constrain the number of work items that can be in progress at any point in time.

Key Stakeholder. A stakeholder who is identified as having a significant stake in the project or program and who holds key responsibilities such as approving requirements or approving changes to product scope.

Lessons Learned. The knowledge gained during a project, which shows how project events were addressed or should be addressed in the future for the purpose of improving future performance.

Measure. The quantity of some element at a point in time or during a specific time duration, such as the number of work months spent on a project during a specific time period, the number of defects uncovered, or the number of customers responding to a survey stating that they were extremely satisfied.

Metric. A set of quantifiable measures used to evaluate a solution or business.

Model. A visual representation of information, both abstract and specific, which operates under a set of guidelines in order to efficiently arrange and convey a lot of information in an efficient manner.

Modeling Language. A set of models and their syntax. Examples include Requirements Modeling Language (RML), Unified Modeling Language (UML), Business Process Modeling Notation (BPMN), and System Modeling Language (SysML).

Monitoring. The process of collecting project performance data, producing performance measures, and reporting and disseminating performance information.

MoSCoW. A technique used for establishing requirement priorities. In this technique, the participants divide the requirements into four categories of must haves, should haves, could haves, and won't haves.

Needs Assessment. The domain of requirement management concerned with understanding business goals and objectives, issues, and opportunities, and recommending proposals to address them.

Negotiation. The process and activities used to resolve disputes through consultations between involved parties.

Nonfunctional Requirements. Requirements that express properties that the product is required to have, including interface, environment, and quality attribute properties.

Objective. Something toward which work is to be directed, a strategic position to be attained, a purpose to be achieved, a result to be obtained, a product to be produced, or a service to be performed. In requirements management, objectives are quantifiable outcomes that are desired from a product, result, or service.

Observation. An elicitation technique that provides a direct way of obtaining information about how a process is performed or a product is used by viewing individuals in their own environment performing their jobs or tasks and carrying out processes.

Open-Ended Question. A question that allows the responder to answer in any way desired.

Opportunity. A risk that would have a positive effect on one or more project objectives. See also *issue, risk,* and *threat.*

Opportunity Analysis. A study of the major facets of a potential opportunity to determine the viability of successfully launching a new product or service.

Opportunity Cost. The loss of value that could be realized in other actions or alternatives, if the current action is pursued.

Participant. One who participates in a group activity, such as focus groups or facilitated workshops.

Persona. An archetype user representing a set of similar end users described with their goals, motivations, and representative personal characteristics.

Phase. See *project phase.*

Portfolio. Projects, programs, subportfolios, and operations managed as a group to achieve strategic objectives. See also *program* and *project.*

Portfolio Management. The centralized management of one or more portfolios to achieve strategic objectives.

Portfolio Manager. The person or group assigned by the performing organization to establish, balance, monitor, and control portfolio components in order to achieve strategic business objectives. See also *program manager* and *project manager.*

Predictive Life Cycle. A form of project life cycle in which the project scope, and the time and cost required to deliver that scope, are determined as early in the life cycle as possible.

Problem. An internal or external environment of an organization that is causing detriment to the organization, for example, lost revenue, dissatisfied customers, delays in launching new products, or noncompliance with government regulations.

Problem Domain. The area or context surrounding the problem that is currently under analysis.

Procedure. An established method of accomplishing a consistent performance or result. A procedure typically can be described as the sequence of steps that will be used to execute a process.

Process. A systematic series of activities directed toward causing an end result such that one or more inputs will be acted upon to create one or more outputs.

Process Flow. A business analysis model that visually shows the steps taken in a process by a human user as it interacts with an implementation. A set of steps taken by a system can be shown in a similar model, a system flow.

Product. An artifact that is produced, is quantifiable, and can be either an end item in itself or a component item. Products are also referred to as materials or goods. See also *deliverable.*

Product Backlog. See *backlog.*

Product Scope. The features and functions that characterize a product, service, or result.

Program. A group of related projects, subprograms, and program activities that are managed in a coordinated way to obtain benefits not available from managing them individually. See also *portfolio* and *project.*

Program Manager. The person authorized by the performing organization to lead the team or teams responsible for achieving program objectives. See also *portfolio manager* and *project manager.*

Project. A temporary endeavor undertaken to create a unique product, service, or result. See also *portfolio* and *program.*

Project Charter. A document issued by the project initiator or sponsor that formally authorizes the existence of a project and provides the project manager with the authority to apply organizational resources to project activities.

Project Life Cycle. The series of phases that a project passes through from its initiation to its closure.

Project Management Plan. The document that describes how the project will be executed, monitored and controlled, and closed.

Project Manager. The person assigned by the performing organization to lead the team that is responsible for achieving the project objectives. See also *portfolio manager* and *program manager.*

Project Phase. A collection of logically related project activities that culminates in the completion of one or more deliverables.

Project Schedule. An output of a schedule model that presents linked activities with planned dates, durations, milestones, and resources.

Project Scope. The work performed to deliver a product, service, or result with the specified features and functions.

Project Stakeholder Management. Includes the processes required to identify all people or organizations impacted by a project, analyzing stakeholder expectations and impact on the project, and developing appropriate management strategies for effectively engaging stakeholders in project decisions and execution.

Project Team. A set of individuals who support the project manager in performing the work of the project to achieve its objectives.

Prototypes. A method of obtaining early feedback on requirements by providing a working model of the expected product before actually building it.

Regulation. A requirement imposed by a governmental body. These requirements can establish product, process, or service characteristics, including applicable administrative provisions that have government-mandated compliance.

Report Table. A business analysis model that documents in a tabular format all of the requirements necessary to develop a single report.

Requirement. A condition or capability that is required to be present in a product, service, or result to satisfy a contract or other formally imposed specification.

Requirements Analysis. The process of examining, breaking down, and synthesizing information to further understand it, complete it, and improve it.

Requirements Attribute. A property of a requirement used to store descriptive information about the requirement, such as last change date, author, source, etc.

Requirements Documentation. A description of how individual requirements meet the business need for the project.

Requirements Elicitation. The activity of drawing out information from stakeholders and other sources for the purpose of further understanding the needs of the business, to address a problem or opportunity and the stakeholder's preferences and conditions for the solution that will address those needs.

Requirements Elicitation and Analysis. The domain of business analysis concerned with the iterative work to plan, prepare, and conduct the elicitation of information from stakeholders and to analyze, model, and document the results of that work with the objective of defining a set of requirements in sufficient detail to enable the purchase or build of the preferred solution or refinement of processes to achieve the business objective.

Requirements Life Cycle. The flow or life of a requirement throughout a project or program. The requirements life cycle is managed by assigning an attribute or qualifier onto the requirement to depict the requirement state at a specified point in time.

Requirements Management Plan. A component of the project or program management plan that describes how requirements will be analyzed, documented, and managed. See also *project management plan.*

Requirements Traceability Matrix. A grid that links product requirements from their origin to the deliverables that satisfy them.

Requirements Verification. The process of reviewing requirements and models to ensure they meet quality standards. Verification is performed to ensure that requirements are constructed properly and that models conform to the proper use of modeling notation.

Responder. Any participant or person from whom information is gathered by means of elicitation.

Return on Investment (ROI). The percent return on an initial project or program investment, calculated by taking the projected average of all net benefits and dividing them by the initial cost.

Risk. An uncertain event or condition that, if it occurs, has a positive or negative effect on one or more project objectives. See also *issue, opportunity,* and *threat.*

Role. A defined function to be performed by a project team member, such as testing, filing, inspecting, or coding.

Root Cause Analysis. An analytical technique used to determine the basic underlying reason that causes a variance or a defect or a risk. A root cause may underlie more than one variance or defect or risk.

Scenario. A case of usage of a solution often manifested as a concrete example of a use case or user story or several functional requirements specified in the sequence in which they occur.

Schedule. See *project schedule.*

Scope. The sum of the products, services, and results to be provided as a project. In requirements management, scope is defined as the boundary for the products, services, or results. See also *project scope* and *product scope.*

Scope Creep. The uncontrolled expansion to a product or project scope without adjustments to time, cost, and resources.

Scope Model. A type of model that identifies the boundaries of the project, program, product, and/or system under analysis. A context diagram is one example of a scope model.

Scrum. A type of adaptive life cycle where a product is built in small incremental portions and each cycle of development builds upon the last version of the product.

Situation. A condition that may be an internal problem or external opportunity that forms the basis of a business need and might result in a project or program to address the condition.

SMART Goals. Goals that are well-written to meet the quality criteria of being specific, measurable, achievable, relevant, and time-bounded.

Solution Evaluation. The domain of requirements management concerned with the activities to validate a solution that is about to be or that has already been implemented.

Solution Requirement. A requirement that describes the features, functions, and characteristics of a product, service, or result that will meet the business and stakeholder requirements. Solution requirements are further grouped into functional and nonfunctional requirements.

Sponsor. An individual or a group that provides resources and support for the project, program, or portfolio, and is accountable for enabling success. See also *stakeholder.*

Stakeholder. An individual, group, or organization that may affect, be affected by, or perceive itself to be affected by a decision, activity, or outcome of a project, program, or portfolio. See also *sponsor.*

Stakeholder Analysis. A technique of systematically gathering and analyzing quantitative and qualitative information to determine whose interests should be taken into account throughout the project.

Stakeholder Identification. The process of determining the stakeholders impacted by a business problem or opportunity.

Stakeholder Register. A project document including the identification, assessment, and classification of project stakeholders.

Stakeholder Requirement. A requirement that describes the need of a stakeholder or stakeholder group.

State Diagram. A business analysis model that visually shows how an object moves between different states. This model helps to show the life cycle of an object in a solution.

State Table. A business analysis model that shows all of the possible states of an object and all of the valid transitions. This model helps to enumerate all possible states and possible transitions.

SWOT Analysis. Analysis of strengths, weaknesses, opportunities, and threats of an organization, project, or option.

System Interface Table. A business analysis model that documents the requirements for the connections between each interfacing system involved in a project, including how they are connected and what information flows between them.

Technique. A defined systematic procedure employed by a human resource to perform an activity to produce a product or result or deliver a service, and that may employ one or more tools.

Technology Feasibility. An analysis to determine the extent to which a technology exists in an organization to support a potential solution and if not present, how feasible it would be to acquire and operate the needed technology.

Template. A partially completed document in a predefined format that provides a defined structure for collecting, organizing, and presenting information and data.

Threat. A risk that would have a negative effect on one or more project objectives. See also *issue, opportunity,* and *risk.*

Traceability. Traceability provides the ability to track product requirements from their origin to the deliverables that satisfy them.

Traceability and Monitoring. The domain of requirements management concerned with building and maintaining the traceability matrix to manage requirements and product scope, baselining the product requirements, assessing impacts of proposed requirement changes, and managing the required updates to the requirements and other requirements management deliverables once proposed changes are approved.

Traceability Matrix. See *requirements traceability matrix.*

Transition Requirements. Requirements that are the temporary capabilities, such as data conversion and training requirements, needed to transition from the current as-is state to the future state.

Use Case. An analysis model that describes a flow of actor-system interactions and boundaries for those interactions, including trigger, initiating and participating actors, and preconditions and post conditions.

Use Case Diagram. A business analysis model that shows all of the in-scope use cases for a project and which actors have a part in those use cases.

User Interface Flow. A business analysis model that shows the specific pages or screens of an application and how a user can navigate between them.

User Story. A one or two sentence description, written from the viewpoint of the actor, describing what function is needed. A user story usually takes the form of "as an <actor>, I want to <function>, so that I can <benefit>."

Validation. The assurance that a product, service, or system meets the needs of the customer and other identified stakeholders. It often involves acceptance and suitability with external customers. Contrast with *verification.*

Value Engineering. An approach used to optimize project life cycle costs, save time, increase profits, improve quality, expand market share, solve problems, and/or use resources more effectively.

Verification. The evaluation of whether or not a product, service, or system complies with a regulation, requirement, specification, or imposed condition. It is often an internal process. Contrast with *validation.*

Weighted Criteria. A technique used to help support objective decision making. It uses a weighted ranking matrix to compare alternatives and their weighted scores in order to evaluate decision options. See also *weighted ranking matrix.*

Weighted Ranking Matrix. A table used in decision making that combines pair matching of all alternatives with weighted criteria to add objectivity when formulating a decision or recommendation. Each alternative is compared with every other alternative on the basis of weighted criteria, and the resulting scores are added together to determine the preferred choice.

Work Breakdown Structure (WBS). A hierarchical decomposition of the total scope of work to be carried out by the project team to accomplish the project objectives and create the required deliverables.

Work Product. An output produced as a result of some completion of work that is required for a short-term purpose and not required to be monitored and maintained on an ongoing basis.

INDEX